Julía Alvarez

JULIA ALVAREZ

Writing a New Place on the Map

❧

KELLI LYON JOHNSON

UNIVERSITY OF NEW MEXICO PRESS

ALBUQUERQUE

See page 180 for complete list of copyright credits.

LIBRARY OF CONGRESS CATALOGING-IN-PUBLICATION DATA

Johnson, Kelli Lyon, 1969–
    Julia Alvarez : writing a new place on the map / Kelli Lyon Johnson.
      p. cm.
    Includes bibliographical references and index.
    ISBN 0-8263-3651-5 (alk. paper)
    1. Alvarez, Julia—Criticism and interpretation.
    2. Women and literature—United States—History—20th century.
    3. Dominican Republic—In literature. 4. Dominican Americans in literature.
    5. Immigrants in literature. I. Title.
      PS3551.L845Z74 2005
      818 .540—dc22
                  2005011097

DESIGN AND COMPOSITION: *Mina Yamashita*

CONTENTS

Acknowledgments

I would like to express sincere appreciation to Ibis Gómez-Vega, Amy Levin, and Diana Swanson for their generosity with time, insights, and inspiration during the completion of the early version of this project. Deborah De Rosa also provided valuable advice and support for this manuscript and related activities. Jan Arwood and Theresa Laskos kindly supported its production as well. These women have all been great mentors and friends. The staff at the Newberry Library was particularly helpful in the selection of early printed and manuscript maps of Hispaniola and of early printed atlases and descriptions of the island and the Caribbean region. The Interlibrary Loan staff at both Northern Illinois University's Founders Memorial Library and Miami University's Rentschler and King Libraries at Miami University tirelessly sought books and articles on my behalf, for which I owe great thanks. And especially to my husband, Martin Johnson, who read every word of this manuscript more than once and offered his words of advice and support, I am grateful. ⌒

INTRODUCTION

Mapping a New Country

I am not a Dominican writer.

Nor am I a norteamericana.

That's why I describe myself as a Dominican American writer. That's not just a term. I'm mapping a country that's not on the map, and that's why I'm trying to put it down on paper.

—Julia Alvarez, *Something to Declare*

Since 1991 and the success of *How the García Girls Lost Their Accents*, Julia Alvarez has become one of the most widely read and admired contemporary U.S. Latina writers. The acclaimed author of four novels, three collections of poetry, a book of essays, two novels for young readers, and two children's books, she ranks among the handful of contemporary authors whose works make both best seller lists and university syllabi. And while her writings are required reading in many high schools, they have also inspired a large body of scholarly articles. Yet, this book provides the first extended analysis of all of Alvarez's works, which, despite their diversity, address a coherent set of issues that are becoming increasingly crucial in contemporary American literature. Perhaps most importantly, Alvarez poses the problem of how we are to understand and represent identity within the multiple migrations that characterize an increasingly global society. By "mapping a country that's not on the map," Alvarez, a Dominican immigrant forced into exile in the United States, is undertaking a journey that places her at the forefront of contemporary American letters.

The question of identity and agency is particularly acute for women, postcolonial peoples, and others upon whom an identity has traditionally been imposed. Given Alvarez's success, both commercial and artistic, a variety of groups have claimed her as a member of their communities: as woman, ethnic, exile, diaspora, Caribbean, Dominican, Latina, and American. In the keynote address at a conference for Caribbean Studies, Doña Aída Cartagena Portalatín, "the grand woman of letters in the Dominican Republic" (*Something* 171) gently chides Alvarez for writing in English. "Come back to your country, to your language," she tells Alvarez. "You are a Dominican" (171). By conflating linguistic, national, and cultural identity, Portalatín underscores the importance of these factors for constructing a literary tradition that includes displaced writers like Alvarez, who quite consciously has not adopted for writing the language of her country of origin.

In response to such comments, Alvarez has asserted her own self-definition as both (and neither) Dominican and American by writing "a new place on the map" (*Something* 173). Placing herself among a multiethnic group of postcolonial authors who write in English— "Michael Ondaatje in Toronto, Maxine Hong Kingston in San Francisco, Seamus Heaney in Boston, Bharati Mukherjee in Berkeley, Marjorie Agosín in Wellesley, Edwidge Danticat in Brooklyn" (173)— Alvarez, like these authors, has altered contemporary American literature by stretching the literary cartography of the Americas. These authors have brought, through their writings, their own countries of origin into a body of work in which the word *American* expands across continents and seas and begins to recapture its original connotation.

Alvarez has also claimed membership among a *comunidad* of U.S. Latina writers—Sandra Cisneros, Ana Castillo, Judith Ortiz Cofer, Lorna Dee Cervantes, Cherríe Moraga, Helena María Viramontes, and Denise Chávez—despite her fears that "the cage of a definition" will enclose her writing "with its 'Latino subject matter,' 'Latino style,' 'Latino concerns'" (169). Like these authors, Alvarez seeks to write women into a postcolonial tradition of literature that has historically excluded women, particularly in writings of exile. To counter imposed definitions and historical silences, Alvarez has found that "the best way to define myself is through stories and poems" (169). The space that

Alvarez maps is thus a narrative space: the site of her emerging cartography of identity and exile.

Julia Alvarez was born on March 27, 1950, in the United States where she lived for the first three months of her life before her parents returned to the Dominican Republic,[1] where her "childhood history" is set (*Something* 116). Her family was forced to flee the politically troubled country in August of 1960 because of her father's role in a failed plot to overthrow the dictatorship of Rafael Leonidas Trujillo. This flight and Trujillo's role in it reappear throughout Alvarez's writings, allowing her to explore the personal, familial, and political consequences of exile, particularly for women. Confronted with a new world in New York City, Alvarez immediately began her project of mapping her new country, and thus a new identity, by "put[ting] it down on paper" (173) in English, her newly claimed "portable homeland." After attending college and completing a master's degree at Middlebury College in Vermont, Alvarez found herself as a sort of itinerant poet, driving across the United States and teaching poetry in elementary schools, nursing homes, community centers, and colleges.

Beginning with her exile, these multiple migrations inform Alvarez's pervasive concern with movement, place, and writing. Her first book of poetry, *Homecoming*, was published in 1984, but she found her widest audience in 1991 with the publication of the best-selling novel, *How the García Girls Lost Their Accents*. In 1994, *In the Time of the Butterflies* secured her place in American letters. After spending some years teaching at Middlebury, Alvarez left academia and now divides her time between Vermont and the Dominican Republic, where she and her husband own and manage a coffee farm,[2] dedicating her energies there not only to cooperative coffee farming but also to local literacy and education.[3] The places of Alvarez's life inform the *mestizaje* of her work, a linguistic and cultural multiplicity that reveals the truth of the words of Palestinian American poet Naomi Shihab Nye, "Where we live in the world/ is never one place" (41).

Mestizaje has historically had at its foundation a concern with race. The word has been reclaimed and redefined by Latino/a writers and critics to include cultural heritage. Alvarez's conception of mestizaje emerges not out of the word's racial connotation, but more out of an exploration of contact and connection. Mestizaje, as Alvarez writes it, resonates in Gloria Anzaldúa's definition of identity, which she has described in an interview: "I think identity is an arrangement or series of clusters, a kind of stacking or layering of selves, horizontal and vertical layers, the geography of selves made up of the different communities you inhabit" (238). The focus on community has particular relevance for a cartography of identity in exile. Alvarez thus advocates the multiplicity of experience, place, and belonging as she draws together not only myriad races but also classes, languages, genders, nations, and cultures in the literature of the Americas. Alvarez maps that multiplicity through narratives of homeland, family, and identity.

Alvarez's map also suggests the significance of her work to postcolonial analyses of exploration and conquest. In contemporary postcolonial discourses, mapping—not just a process of putting ink on paper but also a political project of appropriation and territorialization—functions as a metaphor for colonization, domination, and oppression, while at the same time it represents anticolonial practices of decolonization and transculturation. Through this powerful topos of postcolonial writing, Alvarez has created a geography of identity entextualized in her body of work, joining theory and story across multiple genres to create an alternative map of identity and culture. In *The History of Cartography*, J. B. Harley and David Woodward argue that "[t]he social history of maps, unlike that of literature, art, or music, appears to have few genuinely popular alternative, or subversive, modes of expression. Maps are preeminently a language of power, not of protest" (398). Alvarez's writings, however, demonstrate developing alternatives to traditional maps and suggest the significance of her mapping project to postcolonial writings of the Americas in general. In the same way that maps have been deployed to oppress indigenous inhabitants of countries with colonial histories, maps can be used to reclaim and redefine territory and nationhood, as Alvarez does by claiming her own multiple identities, nations, and languages.

Alvarez's interest in mapping narrative space situates her within much contemporary critical and theoretical work marked by cartographic terminology—place, site, location, position, zone, frontier, territory, terrain, center, margin, and border. This language suggests a kind of positional deixis, in which the words' connotations and denotations are transformed according to subject and object relations.[4] As metaphors, these terms lend spatial imagery to a locational politics of identity and provide a method for describing standpoint or geographical positionality in theory and literature. Affirming Adrienne Rich's assertion that "[a] place on the map is a place in history" (212), feminist theorists have been particularly interested in maps. Feminist geographers and critics have noted that maps not only reinforce traditional paradigms of the landscape as female, but they also represent masculine space, a means of containing and constraining the spaces of the Other(s) in the geographies of contact.

Maps represent spaces that are primarily conceived and defined using borders or boundaries. Geographer Doreen Massey in *Space, Place, and Gender* sees these borders as "culturally masculine" insofar as they fulfill "the need for the security of boundaries, the requirement of such a defensive counter-positional definition of identity" (7). Maps are indeed culturally masculine, emerging out of patriarchal traditions of definition, control, and representation. Such boundaries define who can claim membership in any given group and who is excluded from doing so. Moreover, Massey argues, borders serve "to secure the identity of places," which in turn are attempts "to stabilize the meaning of particular envelopes of space-time" (5). Mapping colonial "discoveries," then, serves both to justify and claim conquests in order to ward off counterclaims; similarly, maps have historically served to create and stabilize knowledge of the previously unknown during the early years of colonization in the Americas. In this sense, not only is the physical space of the world constructed through mapping, but so is knowledge.

Serving masculinist needs for defining and controlling space, borders also control knowledge. In *Mappings*, her own work on borders, Susan

Stanford Friedman suggests that "[b]orders between individuals, genders, groups, and nations erect categorical walls between identities," creating a world in which identity is "unthinkable without some sort of imagined or literal boundary" (3). Borders thus become the means through which both the world itself and its inhabitants are constructed. The very nature of these borders requires that all spaces be closed; Alvarez, however, resists these closed spaces through narrative structure and point of view. Her novel *How the García Girls Lost Their Accents* moves backward in time through the voices of several narrators, as does her novel *In the Name of Salomé*. Alvarez's narratives are thus never closed but instead continually transformed through historical and cultural change and through reader interaction with the text itself.

Border-talk, writes Friedman, "is everywhere—literal and figurative, material and symbolic" (3). Gloria Anzaldúa in *Borderlands/La Frontera* has created a theoretical model of borders in which she celebrates the liberatory position of the borderlands while simultaneously recognizing the danger of border crossing. The borderland Anzaldúa describes is *una herida abierta*—an open wound—a place "where the Third World grates against the first and bleeds. And before a scab forms it hemorrhages again, the lifeblood of two worlds merge to form a third country—a border culture" (25). Anzaldúa's concern with figurative and real borderlands—the national border between the United States and Mexico—evokes a physical and metaphorical space of contestation, a special geographical zone of both oppression and resistance. The Caribbean, however, as a geographical region, defies such spatial metaphors; it does not share a border with the United States, nor do most Caribbean countries share physical borders with one another. Traditional border theories are thus inadequate modes of analysis for Alvarez's writing, which incorporates instead a more fluid and relational vision of identity than the stark line of a border.

Another problem with border theories is that borders, even in multiple numbers, are binary, dividing Same from Different. We are on one side; They are on the Other. Borders keep people in as well as out; they enact enclosure. Moreover, borders have long been used to define and limit women's lives. The borders around women's space—both the physical spaces women inhabit and the psychological and social space by which women are defined—are male-created and male-enforced, and paradoxically, notes Gillian Rose, women become simultaneously prisoners in and exiled from the spaces they inhabit (150). The domestic space of the home, for example, confines women to certain roles, behaviors, and locations as it has become defined as a woman's space since industrialization in the nineteenth century. As feminist scholars have suggested, however, women's autonomy is limited or even absent in that space because men have traditionally overseen the physical, emotional, and, especially, financial activities of the home, a situation that essentially exiles women from roles of authority or power.

Moreover, women who transgress borders established for them—social, political, sexual—often suffer violent consequences. As Anzaldúa has pointed out, "[T]respassers will be raped, maimed, strangled, gassed, shot" (25). Women's space has therefore been constructed through violence. For Alvarez, that violence lies in both the colonial history of the Dominican Republic and the country's series of *caudillo* strongmen and dictators, all of whom used violence to control and shape the landscape of the island and its peoples. Alvarez simultaneously recognizes and resists such violence when she exposes and then rewrites Trujillo's concerted efforts to create a national narrative of identity and history in the Dominican Republic. That she enacts that agency through women characters—the Mirabal sisters—reveals her understanding of the roles women have played in colonial contests for space; controlling women—particularly their labor in both modes of production and reproduction—has long served such projects.

Like Anzaldúa, Homi Bhabha imagines a contestatory space between the two sides of a border, the borderlands where *"something begins its presencing"* (Bhabha, *Location* 5). That space, however, may be difficult to locate on a physical plane and, therefore, within human experience. In contrast, Alvarez's narrative space, instead of existing solely as a metaphor, exists in a physical space—in the novel, the poem, the essay. This narrative space, however, relies not on a crossing-over of borders imposed from without, but rather on an accumulation, a drawing together, of identities and experiences. Alvarez erases borders imposed from the outside, transcends the artificial borders constructed around the spaces she inhabits—Dominican, American, woman, Latina—and includes, rather than excludes, the multiple aspects of her identity.

Alvarez herself conceives of the Caribbean as "a string of islands, a sieve of the continents, north and south, a sponge, as most islands are, absorbing those who come and go, whether indios in canoas from the Amazon, or conquistadores from Spain, or African princes brought in chains in the holds of ships to be slaves, or refugees from China or Central Europe or other islands" (*Something* 175). Alvarez's vision of the Caribbean echoes that of Antonio Benítez-Rojo, who writes in *The Repeating Island* that "as a meta-archipelago [the Caribbean] has the virtue of having neither a boundary nor a center" (4), a perspective of the region that opposes binary constructions of center/margin as well as nationalist constructions of belonging and exclusion. This understanding of the Caribbean requires a theory independent of the border paradigm, such as Alvarez provides.

Alvarez's positionality also transcends physical geographic description—she is neither and both a Dominican and a *norteamericana*—and again concurs with Benítez-Rojo, who argues that "[t]o persevere in the attempt to refer the culture of the Caribbean to geography—other than to call it a meta-archipelago—is a debilitating and scarcely productive project" (24). He rejects a land-based theory of geography in favor of an aquatic paradigm of movement and fluidity, an approach embraced by other Caribbean scholars as well, particularly Kamau Brathwaite, who coined the term "tidalectics"[5] in reference to Caribbean theory (DeLoughrey 19), and Edouard Glissant, who sees the Caribbean as "an open sea. It does not impose one culture, it radiates diversity" (261). The difficulty of using a border theory in the Caribbean points to the need for theoretical mestizaje in postcolonial criticism that grants agency to writers and allows them to write theory from within—not imposed from without—and create a paradigm for reading their own work.[6] Alvarez provides just such an approach to the narrative space of her writing and explicitly rejects mapping that distills or simplifies space and experience. She instead writes a mestizaje that accumulates—across nation, language, identity, gender, and genre—rather than integrates, and thus obscures, its multiple elements.

Alvarez thus offers a compelling vision of both self and community that rejects the paradigm of hybridity as a means of understanding postcolonial, exile, and ethnic literature. Hybridity has emerged as the dominant paradigm for the interpretation and theory of postcolonial literature and culture. The word, however, has experienced a certain loosening of meaning that has resulted in its application to any number of phenomena, from popular religiosity to linguistic code-switching to music. Hybridity has traditionally referred to interchange between two discrete entities—particularly plants or people—and has evolved to describe any kind of interconnection or transfer of culture, language, race, nation, or identity. Perhaps because of its pervasiveness, this concept is among the most contested in postcolonial studies. A growing number of scholars have objected to both the concept and especially the term insofar as hybridity risks reiterating the melting-pot ideology (Piper 16) and colonial discourses of racism and miscegenation, as Robert Young points out in *Colonial Desire*. By "reinvoking this concept," Young argues, "we are utilizing the vocabulary of the Victorian extreme right as much as the notion of an organic process of the grafting of diversity into singularity" (10). Like mapping, hybridity has traditionally been fundamentally reductive. Hybridity implies cultural erasure, which risks rendering invisible the elements that comprise what is hybrid; as a result, those elements disappear from historical, literary, and cultural maps and become lost to memory.

As Isabel Carrera Suárez points out in "Hyphens, Hybridities, and Mixed-Race Identities," people with hyphenated identities, such as Dominican-American or Japanese-Canadian, do not necessarily enjoy the benefits of belonging to cultures on both sides of the hyphen. The hybrid condition, she writes, "often involves personal and social pain, unchosen, unprivileged. No matter how 'Canadian' a condition, it is still perceived by many as foreign to the country, particularly so if race is involved, and rejections of hybridity as a hopeful theory are thus well-grounded" (29). Hybridity in general resonates with assimilation and may negate the anticolonialist project of independence by masking the origins of what is "hybrid." Moreover, the concept of hybridity suggests not only cultural erasure but also the integration of identity and experience, as if the multiplicity of postcolonial identities could be easily recognized and assimilated.

In place of hybridity, Benítez-Rojo offers the mestizaje of the Caribbean, "not [as] a synthesis, but rather the opposite," suggesting that "mestizaje is nothing more than a concentration of differences" (26). Such an approach to Alvarez's writings suggests the creation of a space that allows for that concentration and accumulation of differences, a narrative space. Alvarez, however, differs from Benítez-Rojo in her insistence on the inclusion of gender as a meaningful determinant of identity and experience. Elizabeth DeLoughrey has written a telling critique of Benítez-Rojo's feminization of the Caribbean region, rejecting Benítez-Rojo's portrayal of the Atlantic as "the painfully delivered child of the Caribbean whose vagina was stretched between continental clamps" (Benítez-Rojo 5), a phrase that, DeLoughrey points out, "employs the usual feminized colonial landscape reminiscent of early colonial narratives" (27). In his efforts "to inscribe a regionalism that does not elide sociocultural, linguistic, and natural difference, yet utilizes the sea cartography as a metaphor for a broader Caribbean identity" (18), Benítez-Rojo reiterates colonial discourses such as that of cartographer Thomas Jefferys who, in 1760, proclaimed Hispaniola to be "the mother of all the *Spanish* colonies in the new world" (3). As with Jefferys, Benítez-Rojo renders the colonial space as maternal, limiting women's participation to conception and birth. What DeLoughrey calls his "problematically gendered symbology" (19) inscribes borders around women's identity, experience, and autonomy with the very ideologies Benítez-Rojo seeks to erase with his own re-reading of the region.

As Alvarez indicates in her desire to map a new country, she resists any description or paradigm that might obscure her multiple identities, celebrating the concentration of differences in her own life and the lives of her female characters. The accumulated differences of the Caribbean provide Alvarez simultaneously with a challenge to the construction of identity and the very tools with which to do so. Rejecting hybridity and its concomitant implication of assimilation, Alvarez demonstrates the dis-integration of women's lives, particularly women in exile and women writers and artists. Alvarez's women characters are mothers and writers, daughters and activists, wives and teachers who inhabit spaces throughout the Americas. Emerging out of these multiple roles and cultures, the dis-integration these women experience is internal and psychological, a failure to fuse the conflicting and contradictory identities, expectations, and roles they face in multiple cultures.

Alvarez is thus concerned with the space where things do not come together—the disjuncture of U.S. Caribbean women's lives—and that disjuncture is the narrative space that Alvarez constructs. That disjunction appears as asymptosy—lines that approach each other without meeting—which characterizes Alvarez's use of voice, structure and experience. There are two ways in which the (en)textualization of experience allows Alvarez to create a narrative space in which women of color discover new possibilities for the asymptotic dis-integration of their lives. First, she asserts the agency denied to Caribbean women in postcolonial theory and criticism. Postcolonial theory, especially where it overlaps with feminist theory, is concerned with agency, particularly in regard to the hybridity paradigm. Lizabeth Paravisini-Gebert offers an important criticism of such postcolonial theories when she contends that her "main difficulty with their approaches is that in their elaborations, agency—however challenged, however deconstructed—rests with the colonizers and their traditions." From such a perspective, "the colonized is perpetually condemned to reaction" (161). By envisioning a space independent of external cartographies, Alvarez retains narrative agency. While Alvarez may describe—and decry—colonialism and its legacy in the Dominican Republic, the Caribbean, and the United States, her ability to initiate her own discursive re-creations of those conditions, events, and people reveals Alvarez as the writer and creator of her own narrative, her own history.

The second accomplishment of Alvarez's construction of a narrative space lies in the anticolonial project of deterritorialization.[7] Deterritorialization, argues Caren Kaplan, "is one term for the displacement of identities, persons, and meanings that is endemic to the postmodern world system" (188). For Alvarez's work, deterritorialization reminds us of the connections between landscape and history, in particular the ways that "territory" has been used to construct knowledge and identity. To remove her work from colonial territories—that is, the islands as they were defined by invading Europeans colonists—Alvarez literally displaces her texts from the colonially defined spaces of the Caribbean and the United States by negating the primacy accorded to territory and territorial constructions of identity. The discursive space Alvarez imagines "disturb[s] the ideological manoeuvres through which 'imagined communities' are given essentialist identities" (Bhabha, "DissemiNation" 300). Absent from Alvarez's space are precisely those essentialist identities—the social constructions of what it means to be Dominican, North American, a woman, and a writer. Deterritorializing her writing and the theories that simultaneously bind it to nation-territories, Alvarez emphasizes the text as the primary location of postcolonial culture and identity.

In the postmodern world, "identity is literally unthinkable without narrative" (Friedman 8), and narrative, like identity, is a process, a becoming, a performance. Narrative space interacts with other spaces—physical, social, ideological, linguistic, religious, and economic—but it remains independent of such spaces insofar as it does not rely on others for the subjectivity contained within it. Because Alvarez's locations—social, political, national, linguistic—are discontinuous and mobile, the narrative space of her writing provides her with the "solid ground" she lacks as a Dominican-born woman living in the United

States. Narrative space is, indeed, the dialogic space that Bakhtin describes,[8] but the dialogue it initiates with the reader and the world proceeds on its own terms, which Alvarez delineates in her explorations of exile, language, history, identity, and memory. In its dialogism, Alvarez's narrative space allows her agency and resists the boundaries and borders of definable, containable spaces. Narrative space for Alvarez is gendered space, gendered in its deterritorialization of women's spaces, in its revelation of the dis-integration of women's lives, and in its realization of the role of creativity and improvisation in the face of such dis-integration.

"The page is where I've learned to put together my different worlds, where I've put down my deepest roots," Alvarez has said. "Maybe because I am an immigrant, I don't feel those deep loyalties to a piece of land or a landscape. But the world of the imagination is the one I feel most at home in. I am a traveler with this portable homeland of the imagination" (Kevane and Heredia 32). The resonance of this journey can be measured by her devoted readership and scholarly analysis. Through narrative Alvarez maps for herself and her readers not a borderland but a homeland. ⌒

THE PARADOX
OF REMEMBERED SPACE

In contemporary postcolonial theory, the tropes of mapping and geography illuminate the significance of space in projects of decolonization, self-determination, and independence. As is apparent in colonial maps of Hispaniola and the Caribbean, allocation and control of territory through mapping have real consequences beyond metaphorical claims for making room for new identities. These consequences include exploitation, slavery, and genocide. Maps have long been taken as transparent, as if they were mere and precise representations of actual space in the world. Alvarez undermines the illusion of transparency in her narrative map by transforming space into a particular place through storytelling. Julia Alvarez's efforts to map a narrative space of mestizaje depend on contests for space. Her narratives must be read against the long tradition of mapping the Caribbean, which has historically been a means of defining and controlling terrain. In her own detailed presentations of the places and spaces of her life, Alvarez reveals the paradox of exile: remembered spaces distort the actual place of the homeland.

The Caribbean's colonial history has much to do with rejections of geographical paradigms of territory as a determinant of identity. The region's long history of geographical definition has suppressed its diversity, which the conception of a "hybrid" Caribbean continues to threaten. Beginning with Christopher Columbus's first sketches, early European maps of the Americas reveal the ideologies that European men both created and reinforced about the Caribbean and its inhabitants. These maps simultaneously claimed, defined, and subjugated the region for European invaders and their home governments and sovereigns. Alvarez instead claims the territories of her own experience for those who have traditionally been excluded from mapmaking and its concomitant access to power. In particular, she maps women's experiences beyond the sexual and reproductive role often ascribed to them in early narratives of the Americas.

These early maps expose the multiple meanings inscribed upon the space of the Americas through text and image. In one early example, a 1632 map of the island of Hispaniola, now divided between the Dominican Republic and Haiti, mapmaker Nicolás de Cardona includes fields, crops, houses, a fort, churches, a river, a tower, and ships entering and exiting the harbor and river. While seeming merely descriptive, this map clearly emphasizes for Europeans that the island can provide spaces for construction—the fort, houses, the church, a guide tower—as well as crops, resources, and access for any number of ships that might navigate through the waters to the capital city of Santo Domingo. This map demonstrates the ways that mapping is an external process that imposes order from without; in contrast, Alvarez draws the interiors of private homes, churches, museums, prisons, and schools, revealing the Dominican Republic from within.

In addition to physical structures, the natural environment had market value to Europeans, and thus to European mapmakers. Geographer, naturalist, and missionary Johannes de Laet similarly promotes the potential wealth of the island in his *Histoire du Nouveau Monde*, published in 1640. In his depiction of Hispaniola, he begins by describing the island's temperature, weather, and guava trees, the apparent interests of a naturalist. He concludes that paragraph, however, with information about how this climate affects the fertile territory and allows it to accommodate both crops and domestic animals. Three paragraphs later he enumerates "les principales richesses" of the island—sugar cane, ginger, coffee, and cows—and notes, "Les habitans Espagnols traitent toutes ces choses avec grand profit" (2). [The Spanish inhabitants profit greatly from all of these things.] Geographer to the King, Nicolas Sanson d'Abbeville includes in his 1656 *Amerique, en Plusieurs Cartes Nouvelles* that in addition to sugar, pastures, and coffee, the island offers gold mines, salt, and beauty. In *The Natural and Civil History of the French Dominions in North and South America*, the influential and prolific map publisher Thomas Jefferys sums up

> the character of the island in these few words. *St. Domingo* has good harbors for trade, the soil is fertile, producing various rich commodities, as well as plenty of cattle, grain, fruits, and vegetables fit for human subsistence. The sea and the mouths of the rivers abound with delicious fish; the shores are covered with the most curious shells; the air is none [*sic*] of the best, and the inhabitants have great wealth, but little religion. (75)

Such maps and their accompanying descriptions defined what was valuable on the island and thus constructed its image for Europeans. These mapmakers viewed the Americas as commodities, which they exploited through marketing to Europeans on the continent who could subsidize future voyages and explorations.

Women were inscribed in these early narratives as both dangerous and valuable, as colonial mapmakers exploited constructions of gender in their descriptions of the "New World."[1] Such constructions are apparent in a 1688 map of the "Archipelague du Mexique," by Venetian cosmographer and globemaker Marco Vincenzo Coronelli. Into the map's cartouche, which generally contains the map's title and mapmaker's name, Coronelli inscribed images from the Genesis story—Eve, Adam, and Satan. Adam and Eve stand on the left side of the cartouche; Eve with breast revealed tugs on Adam's shoulder, and Satan observes them from his position to the right. Such cartographic ornamentation provides as much information as the map itself. Drawings of Adam, Eve, and Satan evoke the idea of Paradise, but it is also a paradise lost because of the wanton sexuality of native women, the dangers of the exotic, and the paganism of the island inhabitants. Jean Baptiste Labat, a Dominican traveler, specifically represents these island inhabitants in his 1722 etchings of both a male and a female "Caraïbe." The man holds weapons while the woman wears jewelry and other adornments, creating and reinforcing masculine discourses of the dangers of the exotic islands as well as the physical beauty—and thus desirability—of their female inhabitants, another marketing ploy for Europeans in their quest for wealth in the West Indies. Alvarez is writing specifically against these discourses as she portrays Caribbean and Caribbean American women as agents of political, social, and economic change. She refuses the hypersexuality of these constructions without denying women's sexual autonomy, as many writers have done since the rise of the novel.

Similar etchings accompany the maps of Nicolas Ponce, which reveal the connection between the islands and their monetary worth. He draws a variety of slaves (*esclaves*), freed women slaves (*affranchies*), and indigenous women working as laundresses (*blanchisseuses*). While in the market performing important public tasks of spending and serving, these women are clothed, but they are otherwise depicted topless, and the laundresses are naked. As Alison Blunt and Gillian Rose have found, "[i]mperialist literature often incorporated sexual imagery to create and sustain the heroic stature of male colonizers who conquered and penetrated dangerous, unknown continents, often characterized by the fertility of both indigenous vegetation and women" (10). These etchings and early maps demonstrate a long tradition of the feminization of the landscape and the sexualization of native and African women. Moreover, the details of these maps provide an important context—in its sense of being "with text"—for Alvarez's writing as she seeks to write atop and against such constructions of Caribbean identity. Alvarez must construct her own space in narrative so that it can be read against the crowded space of five hundred years of history written by men intent on not only describing but also exploiting the Caribbean region.

Early cartographic practices also provide insight into the perpetuation of knowledge about the Americas. William Berry's well-known 1689 *Collection of Maps of the World* draws on the work of others; the title page states that the maps were "described by Sanson[,] corrected and amended by William Berry." Royal geographer Jean Baptiste d'Anville published an atlas in 1727 "dressée sur un grand nombre de Cartes particulières, sur les instructions des Navigateurs et Voyageurs, sur les récits des Historiens Espagnols, qui fournissent des details qu'on n'a point fait entrer dans les cartes." [Based on a large number of special Maps, on the instructions of Navigators and Travelers, on the accounts of Spanish Historians, who have furnished details that have yet to be portrayed on maps.] Similarly, Emmanuel Bowen's 1747 *Complete System of Geography* was "Extracted from Several Hundred Books of TRAVELS and HISTORY" and had preserved "all that is Useful in the Fourth and Last Edition of the COMPLETE GEOGRAPHER, publish'd under the Name of HERMAN MOLL, &c." Bowen has decided what is "useful" for his readers, privileging the masculine traditions of geography as a means of mapping developing markets and thus erasing cultures that he judges to be without market value. Knowledge about the islands and their inhabitants—particularly regarding their religion, sexuality, and material value—have come down through this masculine tradition of geography and cartography so that even contemporary theories of the Caribbean must contend with the racist, sexist statements made by these maps and the men who created them. The paradox of these "remembered spaces" is that they are not remembered at all; instead, they are reproduced from a small number of knowledge makers (cartographers, printers, and publishers) who had never visited the places they constructed for others.

As part of her project to write a new place on the map, Alvarez inscribes the Dominican landscape throughout the whole of her writings. Her first novel, *How the García Girls Lost Their Accents* (1991), begins with Yolanda García, the protagonist, on a return journey from the United States to the Dominican Republic. On the island, "[a]ll around her are the foothills, a dark enormous green, the sky more a brightness than a color. A breeze blows through the palms below, rustling their branches, so they whisper like voices" (12). Yolanda comes to believe that the landscape of the island "is what she has been missing all these years without really knowing that she has been missing it" (12).

Alvarez genders the landscape as well when Yolanda takes a solitary driving trip across the island, against the advice of her family members who feel the country is too dangerous for a woman to travel alone. On her trip, "[t]he rustling leaves of the guava trees echo the warnings of her old aunts: you will get lost, you will get kidnapped, you will get raped, you will get killed" (17). In Yolanda's insistence on driving into the countryside, Alvarez contrasts Yolanda's "American" notions of space and independence with her aunts' ideas about confinement and safety, a split not only between the two countries but also between the two generations. Alvarez's association of the landscape with her aunts' warnings underscores the continued prevalence of male violence that serves to constrain women's spaces and freedom of movement.

The violence of conquest is also apparent in Alvarez's second novel, *In the Time of the Butterflies* (1994). At a Discovery Day party celebrating Columbus's arrival in the Caribbean, one of the main characters, Minerva Mirabal, must spend the evening with the country's despotic and despised dictator, Rafael Trujillo. Although his background is both humble and Haitian, Trujillo pretends a Spanish heritage, a marker of social, economic, and racial superiority in his construction of Dominican national identity. At the celebration, "the Spanish ambassador presents this illustrious descendent of the great Conquistador with yet another medal" (95). When Minerva is forced to dance with Trujillo, he says to her, "Perhaps I could conquer this jewel as El Conquistador conquered our island." When Minerva responds, "I'm afraid I'm not for conquest" (99), her family suffers for her candor. Her father is arrested and held, an internment that ultimately leads to his death. This scene demonstrates Alvarez's awareness of the violent conquest that has shaped the island's colonial history, one that has subjugated women as objects of conquest and written them out of that history except for their sexual and reproductive value. The death of Minerva's father reiterates that conquest insofar as he suffers the retribution for Minerva's claims to autonomy.

In addition to the feminization of the landscape, Alvarez is also aware of the Dominican Republic as a commercial landscape. In *A*

Cafecito Story (2001), a book for "children of all ages," the main character, Joe, tires of his life in Nebraska and looks into taking a trip to the
Dominican Republic. On the Internet, he sees "photos showing barely
clad beauties tossing beach balls with waves surrounding the background" (6), a vision of the country that continues to equate the landscape with women's sexuality. Alvarez reveals this vision for what it is,
however: a capitalist construction reliant on racism, classism, and
exploitation. When Joe arrives in the Dominican Republic, he finds that
"[t]he beach resort is surrounded by a high wall, guards at the
entrances, checking ID cards. No natives are allowed on the grounds
except the service people who wear Aunt Jemima kerchiefs and faux-
Caribbean costumes" (9). Here, spaces are restricted by nationality and,
in particular, by class, as the wall serves as a border keeping people outside of a proscribed space. When Joe decides to see what lies on the
other side of that wall, he takes a trip into the Dominican landscape and
sees another transformation that is the result of capitalism: "As the
truck heads up the narrow, curving road, Joe notices the brown moun-
tainsides, ravaged and deforested, riddled with gullies. The road is
made even more narrow by huge boulders. They must roll down during rainstorms. No trees to hold back the eroding soil" (12). Alvarez is
particularly interested in the environmental destruction wrought by
large coffee corporations, which have destroyed the landscape for profit with little regard for future production or ecological health. The
destruction of the countryside for monetary gain echoes early
European exploitation of the country's natural wealth, and Alvarez
demonstrates that the country continues to be exploited.

In *A Cafecito Story*, Alvarez also emphasizes the changing landscape
of the United States, another result of commercialization and rampant
capitalism, and thus brings together different regions of the Americas
within the narrative. Joe escapes to the Dominican Republic because of
the changing view outside his window of the fields of Nebraska, which
"became parking lots and housing developments, small malls with big
chain stores" (6). When he returns for a visit fifteen years after his move

to the Dominican Republic, "Joe barely recognizes his hometown in Nebraska. There are a lot more houses, a new mall, a truck stop, a strip of fast-food chains" (29). This urban sprawl destroys the family farm in Nebraska in the same way that coffee corporations destroy small coffee farms and local cooperatives in the Dominican Republic. This connection is important for Alvarez's mapping of a new country. In the space of a single story, she brings together both the Dominican and the North American experience and shows not only the differences but also the similarities between her two nations. Most significant, however, is that she does not eclipse the story of either and does not engage in the cultural erasure that has long marked discussions and interpretations of the postcolonial experience. In the same way that colonial culture sought to replace the culture of the Caribbean, so does a "hybrid" Caribbean culture risk replacing the various nations, language, ethnicities, memories, and cultures that have created the Caribbean region.

NARRATIVE SPACE

Narrative has informed recent theoretical efforts to distinguish between space and place. As Amy Kaminsky has suggested, "Physical space is given shape by our telling stories about it (making maps, inventing nations and neighborhoods, and so on)." In this way, "space becomes (like) text" (47). In Alvarez's texts, she maps within a "counter-space"— her narrative space—the multiplicity of places that have defined her and that, in turn, she now seeks to define. Place, writes Paul Carter in *The Road to Botany Bay*, is "space with a history" (xxiv), a conception reinforced by Doreen Massey, who argues that "ideas of place-identity are also always constructed by reference to the past" (8). Yi-Fu Tuan suggests in *Space and Place* that, unlike space, "[p]lace is an organized world of meaning. It is essentially a static concept" (179). Kathleen Kirby similarly argues in *Indifferent Boundaries* that "[p]lace seems to assume set boundaries that one fills to achieve a solid identity" (19). These theorists insist on the static, solid, and historicized nature of place, conceptions that seem antithetical to discussions of migrations, exile, and displacement. I suggest, however, that place is not necessarily the proscribed reality that these scholars suggest; its meaning fluctuates in relation to narrative, and its static dimension has traditionally rested in the dearth of alternatives to a monolithic version of History. When History is the only story available, a place-identity of the region obscures other renderings and versions. Brian Jarvis in *Postmodern Cartographies* sees as inseparable "space/place/landscape and social relations," which are often rendered in narrative. "In other words," Jarvis writes, "all spaces contain stories and must be recognised as the site of an ongoing struggle over meaning and value" (7). Narrative, for many exile writers, has become a primary means of offering other stories that in turn present and create alternative descriptions of their countries of origin.

Space is not merely, or even primarily, a literary problem. Alvarez recognizes the real issues of access to space/s, particularly relevant for those marginalized because of their nationality, gender, race, ethnicity, culture, language, sexual orientation, or religion. Access to space and freedom of movement within and across space are particularly relevant in Alvarez's writings. Because of global migrations—many the forced dis/placements that result from war, genocide, and racism—space is, as Francesco Loriggio suggests, "a major project of our *fin-de-siècle*" (3), echoing Michel Foucault's assertion that "[t]he present epoch will perhaps be above all the epoch of space" (22). Foucault sees our epoch as "one in which space takes for us the form of relations among sites" (23) because of trends of mass migration and movement. I would argue that such movements change the locus of identity formation from a single place to multiple spaces.[2] Alvarez's work in this area—the drawing together of Nebraska and the Dominican Republic, for example, to show similarity in addition to difference—suggests the significance of Foucault's assertion of relationships and interconnections. Alvarez's narrative space functions as one of Foucault's "counter-sites," which he sees as "a kind of effectively enacted utopia in which the real sites, all the other real sites that can be found within the culture, are simultaneously represented, contested, and inverted" (24). Her writings provide just such a location in which to map multiple identities, a mestizaje of self, location, and experience, in order to contest dominant narratives of the Americas.

Henri Lefebvre also envisions counter-sites in *The Production of Space*, in which he argues that space is generative, an "act of creation" that is, "in fact, a process" (34). Viewing space as a process dispels the "illusion of a transparent, 'pure,' neutral space" (292), which allows us to apprehend space as a social phenomenon. Constantly in flux, the social spaces that Lefebvre describes create the possibility of counter-space. Counter-spaces may evolve, for example, "[w]hen a community fights the construction of urban motorways or housing-developments, when it demands 'amenities' or empty spaces for play and encounter" (381–82). Among these counter-spaces lies Alvarez's narrative space, both a generative space she produces by dismantling binary constructions of gender, nation, and race, and a space for the representations, contestations, and inversions that Foucault and Lefebvre envision. As a counter-space, her writings serve to deterritorialize traditional constructions of identity as well.

Feminist geographers and theorists insist on the gendered dimension of space, insofar as it is a social construction. Space is not an "absolute independent dimension," but rather is "constructed out of social relations" (Massey 2), and as such has been coded masculine, apparent in the words we use to describe space—universal, theoretical, conceptual (Massey 9)—which are abstract words long associated with male constructs of knowledge, thought, and reasoning. Feminists recognize that space is not merely an abstract concept but rather is made concrete through ideological processes such as architecture, national borders, and maps. Feminist geographers "have hinted that there are more spaces than meet [the] eye" (Rose 36–37), suggesting multiplicity rather than singularity in constructions of space.

The distinction between place and space informs constructions of hybridity as well. Places as they have been envisioned by postcolonial critics are quantifiable, distinct from one another, and associated with a single identity, whereas space is more amorphous and ambiguous.

The places of Alvarez's writings, then, can be brought together into her narrative space without obscuring any of them through melding or blending into a single, unified location. The relationship between hybridity and space is also useful in an examination of Alvarez's work. As Friedman has argued,

> As a discourse of identity, hybridity often depends materially, as well as figuratively, on movement through space, from one part of the globe to another. This migration through space materializes a movement through different cultures that effectively constitutes identity as the product of cultural grafting. Alternatively, hybridity sometimes configures identity as the superimposition of different cultures in a single space often configured as a borderland, as a site of blending and clashing. (24)

Friedman's description elucidates the context of Alvarez's work as an effort to find something more than "a single space" in which to recreate the multiple migrations apparent in her writings. The space critics have so far envisioned for Alvarez's writing relies on fusion and assimilation, a space that critics see as a location of hybridity.[3] In place of hybridity, Alvarez writes the mestizaje of her experience as a U.S. Caribbean Latina woman writer in exile—accumulated identities that resist hybridic labels such as "Latina" or "Caribbean," which eclipse the other elements of her identity and render invisible certain spaces and places that have shaped her work. Alvarez's mestizaje, inscribed in the multiplicity of her narrative spaces—poetry, essay, novel, children's story— replaces hybridity as a paradigm for rendering those migrations and draws together a multiplicity of places into her writings.

Space and narrative are, then, processes, both of which inform our construction of the world. The narrative space Alvarez creates of her work recalls J. Michael Dash's suggestion that we may view the world "not as terra firma but as a series of intertextual sites," the effect of which is that "geographical space, landscape, and human communities are inscribed with the rhetoric and images of given discursive practices" (22). These discursive practices have long excluded women, the poor, and people of color all over the world. The actual existence of these groups indicates that such discursive paradigms of the world do not reflect "objective reality" but rather have attempted to constitute meaning themselves. As a result, "[t]his reconstructive power of narrative has had profound effects" (Dash 22), which Alvarez interrogates by deploying this reconstructive power in new ways, including the stories long absent from literary constructions of the world.

The notion of a discursive space for Caribbean women writers is not new; in fact, Elaine Savory has identified the "creative space we call Caribbean women's writing," which is not "predictable or easily definable" ("Ex/Isle" 169). H. Adlai Murdoch has similarly suggested that "[a]s far as a feminine Caribbean discourse is concerned, the task of delineating a specific discursive space is doubly difficult," particularly because of "the double subjection by which colonialism exacerbates for women the repressive hierarchies of its authoritarian, hierarchical structures" (62). These descriptions of discursive space point to its conception as a space without a physical location, as if it were metaphorical or mythical—or both. By deploying a physical, pragmatic location in her texts, Alvarez articulates a new theory of her Caribbean experience. She offers alternative visions of conventional spaces—closets, compounds, patios—and multiple narratives of a variety of places—the Dominican Republic, New York City, Nebraska, Vermont—in order to write the mestizaje of her art.

THE PARADOX OF REMEMBERED SPACES

Alvarez explicitly and carefully examines in her writings, particularly in her fiction, the places she has inhabited. Within those places—in particular, New York City, Vermont, and the Dominican Republic—Alvarez explores the space(s) available to her as an exile, as an immigrant, as a woman, as a daughter, as a Latina, and as a writer. She looks at the United States from the perspective of an immigrant, and she looks at the Dominican Republic from the perspective of an exile. The spaces that she remembers from her childhood in both countries turn out to be complex and often contradictory. The close quarters of the dwellings of her childhood in the United States contrast sharply with her memories of the open family compound in the Dominican Republic; however, the freedoms allowed women in the United States oppose the confining roles that Alvarez portrays for Dominican women. Her view of the spaces of these two countries emerges through the lens of gender; she interrogates the boundaries—apparent in customs, traditions, and ideologies—that have traditionally constrained women's lives. It is often through narrative, through storytelling, that Alvarez's women negotiate and transcend such constraints.

How the García Girls Lost Their Accents explores the spaces of the United States that the Garcías face when they flee the Dominican Republic and its dictatorship. They initially live in a "small, dark apartment near Columbia University" (28), a situation that strains the patience of all six family members. Laura García, the García girls' mother, remembers the confinement in the chapter she narrates in the novel's sequel, *¡Yo!* (1997). When the girls would fight at home, confined in their lives in the apartment and in their roles as Latina immigrants, Laura remembers,

> I resorted to locking them in closets. The old-fashioned apartment was full of them, deep closets with glass knobs and those keyholes like in cartoons for detectives to look through and big iron keys with the handle part shaped like a fleur-de-lis. I always used the same four closets, a small one in the girls' bedroom and a big one in mine, the broom closet in the hall, and finally the coat closet in the living room. (29–30)

Although she is not proud of this particular parenting technique, Laura remembers it as the only alternative to the arguing and fighting, the disruption and turmoil, that she remembers from the island under Trujillo from which they had been trying to escape. Moreover, the confinement they experienced in the Dominican Republic—trapped in the family compound surrounded by the secret police and spies—increases in the United States as they are forced into such close quarters because of economic need. Laura recognizes the cruelty of locking the girls in closets—even for a short time while tempers diffused—but her experience in the Dominican Republic leads her to believe it is the only choice. Closets ensure both silence and privacy for the resolution of family problems. Confinement, as we see in Alvarez's writings of Trujillo, is a habit of dictatorship.

Visitors from the Dominican Republic associate the United States with confinement as well, although the complexity of human interaction in these spaces has significant consequences for these visitors. After the Garcías flee the Dominican Republic, they invite one of their maids, Primi, to live with them in New York. Primi's name is a diminutive form of the nickname Primitiva, which Laura had "given" to her when Primi cared for Laura as a child. This name hints at the class stratification so pervasive in the Dominican Republic, a separation that continues among them in the United States when Primi is lodged in the family's basement. When Sarita, Primi's daughter, comes to live with her mother, she stays with her in the basement, and she voices the class discomfort that these stratified spaces suggest. Sarita, who tells her story in ¡Yo!, "felt all the more grateful to Mamá for what she'd been through for five lonely years; imprisoned—that's the way I thought of it—in that house with only Sundays off" (60). Although they are no longer living in a cramped apartment near Columbia, the Garcías offer their maid the least appealing space in their home. Although Primitiva does not complain, her daughter thinks of her as a prisoner, someone living in a small space and constricted by the Garcías' rules. Primitiva is only "free" on Sundays, but she is never free of the basement, the symbol of her social status in the household. Sarita, however, recognizes that the Garcías in the United States are also prisoners of their own wealth because, "in that fancy area of the Bronx, everyone was locked up in a house that had a burglar alarm system and heavy drapes on the windows" (60). The spaces may have grown slightly bigger, but the isolation renders their exile and displacement increasingly painful.

Alvarez describes other spaces in the United States as cramped and confining. The Garcías "moved out of the city to a neighborhood on Long Island so that the girls could have a yard to play in, so Mami said. The little green squares around each look-alike house seemed more like carpeting that had to be kept clean than yards to play in. The trees were no taller than little Fifi" (*García Girls* 151). Not only are the spaces small, but so are the trees, suggesting a neighborhood without a history. They find themselves alone in their own yards, in contrast to the shared family compound that they remember in the Dominican Republic. That the Garcías are girls further increases their confinement. Despite the fact that they are in the United States, "[c]ooped up in those little suburban houses, the rules were as strict as for Island girls" (107). Those strict rules also apply at the boarding school that the girls attend, but they soon learn to circumvent them in their efforts to shed their island identities and the strictures constraining traditional behavior for Dominican women. At boarding school, Yolanda writes,

> [w]e learned to forge Mami's signature and went just about everywhere, to dance weekends and football weekends and snow sculpture weekends. We could kiss and not get pregnant. We could smoke and no great aunt would smell us and croak. We began to develop a taste for the American teenage good life, and soon, Island was old hat, man. (108)

The girls first negotiate their freedom in physical spaces and then through their social and sexual autonomy, metaphorical spaces of womanhood accessible only in escaping the physical confines of the apartment, the school, and even the family.

In other places in these two novels, Alvarez associates freedom with the Dominican Republic. Sarita remembers the freedom of her life in the countryside when she had lived with her grandmother before coming to the United States. Life in the García household was so isolated compared to the island. Even when I lived out in the campo, Abuela and I woke up in the morning and went outside until it was time for bed. Our living room was three rocking chairs under the almond tree facing our neighbors' rocking chairs. The kitchen was a palm roof over a counter of carbon fire where a bunch of women cooked and gossiped together. The toilet was a field on the far side of the river, and the public bath was *in* that river. (*¡Yo!* 59–60)

In the United States, Sarita's only escape is school, a connection that Alvarez frequently makes between access to space and the life of the mind, both manifestations of freedom and autonomy. While Sarita's memories of the spacious Dominican Republic lie with her family in the countryside, the Garcías remember the open spaces of the family compound. Laura says, "Back on the island we lived not as what is here called the nuclear family, which already the name should be a hint that you're asking for trouble cooping up related tempers in the small explosive chambers of each other's attention" as they are forced to do in the United States (*¡Yo!* 21–22). In both Sarita's and Laura's memories, space and family are associated, either providing or limiting freedom according to the landscape of class, gender, and nation. Yolanda similarly describes the compound when she returns to visit the island: "Through well-tended gardens beyond her patio, narrow stone paths diverge. After cake and *cafecitos*, the [female] cousins will disperse down these paths to their several compound houses. There they will supervise cooks in preparing supper for the husbands, who will troop home after Happy Hour" (*García Girls* 7). The garden paths suggest Alvarez's conception of privileged Dominican womanhood; although there are several paths, those paths are narrow and they all lead to the same place—the domestic space of the house where women's roles are proscribed to cooking, childrearing, and household management. This image suggests a theme that runs throughout Alvarez's descriptions of the spaces of the Dominican Republic. They are determined and defined by gender.

In contrast to what they remember about the open spaces of the island, the García girls find that in the United States their behavior—and thus their access to physical and psychological space—is controlled through threats of "island confinement" (*García Girls* 129). After Fifi, the youngest of the teenage daughters, is caught with a baggie of marijuana, her parents send her to live on the island. Her oldest sister predicts, "You'll be climbing these walls before the year is out" (117), referring to the "high stone wall" that surrounds the family compound. That wall is indicative of the constraints that Fifi will experience: chaperones, strict beauty standards, and a new boyfriend—cousin Manuel Gustavo—who dictates to whom she can speak, how she dresses, and appropriate ways to spend her free time. On a return visit, after their father has achieved with Fifi "one successfully repatriated daughter" (117)—a threat to them all—the remaining daughters find Fifi transformed:

> a jangle of bangles and a cascade of beauty parlor curls held back on one side very smartly with a big gold barrette. She has darkened her lashes with black mascara so that her eyes stand out as if she were slightly startled at her good luck. Fifi—who used to wear her hair in her trademark, two Indian braids that she pinned up in the heat like an Austrian milkmaid. Fifi—who always made a point of not wearing makeup or fixing herself up. Now she looks like the *after* person in one of those *before-after* makeovers in magazines. (117)

Coupled with Fifi's new appearance is Manuel Gustavo's refusal to wear a condom, threatening not only their developing sexual relationship but also Fifi's independence, as the specter of pregnancy overshadows any future plans she might have outside of marriage and motherhood. The three sisters stage a "revolution" and contrive a situation in which Fifi and Manuel are discovered alone, a violation of "Rule *número dos*: Girls are not to be left unchaperoned with their *novios*" (128). The immediate result of Fifi's indiscretion is that all four girls must return to the

United States—far from Manuel Gustavo—and it is at that moment that they discover the paradox of their exile identity and experience. About to be returned to New York,

> [w]e were free at last, but here, just at the moment the gate swings open, and we can fly the coup, Tía Carmen's love revives our old homesickness [for the island]. It's like this monkey experiment Carla read about in her clinical psychology class. These baby monkeys were kept in a cage so long, they wouldn't come out when the doors were finally left open. (131)

The paradox of this constrained space is that its relationship to the family complicates the girls' identities, beliefs, and desires.

Even when not in violation of household rules, the García girls spend their summers in the Dominican Republic, trips that are supposed to reinforce their identities not only as Dominicans but also as proper young ladies. They return as teenagers with North American consciousnesses, the kind they acquired in the late 1960s, so the girls have trouble adjusting to Dominican beliefs about women's roles. Soon after they arrive, they give up trying to assert women's rights among their Dominican cousins, aunts, and uncles. All four girls remember that in response to sexist remarks, "[f]or the benefit of an invisible sisterhood, since our aunts and girl cousins consider it very unfeminine for a woman to go around demonstrating for her rights, Yoyo sighs and all of us roll our eyes. We don't even try anymore to raise consciousness here. It'd be like trying for cathedral ceilings in a tunnel" (*García Girls* 121). This spatial image illustrates both women's confinement in the "tunnel" of tradition in the Dominican Republic and the lack of support—necessary for high ceilings—that women lend to one another in demonstrating for their rights. "Once," the girls say, in a chapter written from their collective point of view, "we did take on Tía Flor, who indicated her large house, the well-kept grounds, the stone Cupid who had been re-routed so that his mouth spouted water. 'Look at me, I'm a queen,' she argued. 'My husband has to go to work every day. I can sleep until noon, if I want. I'm going to protest for my rights?'" (121). This attitude is not surprising from Tía Flor, whose socioeconomic class places her among those Dominicans who wish to preserve tradition and, thus, their privilege. Dominicans of this class often stress their Spanish heritage, linking their country with the *conquistadores* rather than the indigenous peoples or the slaves whom colonists forced to the island from Africa. One aunt greets Yolanda's friend, Dexter, with the words, "Welcome to the land Columbus loved best" (¡*Yo!* 197), words that demonstrate pride in their colonial heritage. Women like Tía Flor, men like their cousin Manuel Gustavo, and the wall that surrounds the family compound all serve to create and reinforce the enclosure of women's spaces. The open spaces that the girls "remember" of their childhood lives on the de la Torre family compound contradict the actual experiences of Fifi and Tía Flor.

The wall surrounding the family compound reflects not only gendered constraints but also the political turmoil on the island. Yolanda had always "believed as a child [that the wall] was there to keep the sea back in case during a hurricane it rose up to the hillside the family houses were built on" (*García Girls* 10). Looking at the wall as an adult, she sees that the family employs "a private guard" with a "gun swung over his shoulder" (10). This wall represents the oppression suffered by all Dominicans during Trujillo's dictatorship, 1930–1961, and during the subsequent regimes that struggled for power in the wake of his assassination. Once serving to keep a certain class of people outside, the wall under Trujillo's regime served to lock the de la Torre family inside. One de la Torre cousin, Lucinda, remembers in ¡*Yo!* that just after Trujillo's death

> things had gotten really bad on the island. We were having one revolution after another as if we couldn't kick the habit of murdering each other even after our dictator was gone. Anyhow, for a couple of years, schools were all but shut down. I remember a lot of nights sleeping under the bed on account of the stray bullets shattering the windows. (38)

Such conditions suggest "a pretty claustrophobic life in that family compound" (38). The oppressive spaces of violence reveal the paradox of many Latin American and Caribbean struggles for freedom in the wake of colonialism.

The confining spaces that result from political instability and violence emerge in other of Alvarez's depictions of the Dominican Republic. *Before We Were Free* (2002) is a book for young adult readers that focuses on the same period that Lucinda briefly describes: the aftermath of Trujillo's assassination. The protagonist of the book, Anita de la Torre, is a cousin of the Garcías, the younger sister of Lucinda, both of whom remain in the Dominican Republic after the Garcías flee to the United States. After Anita's father and brother are implicated in Trujillo's assassination, Lucinda is sent to the United States, and Anita and her mother must go into hiding in the home of an employee of the Italian embassy. The Mancinis hide Anita and her mother in the walk-in closet attached to their bedroom. Mrs. Mancini shows them "the accommodations": "Here is the dining room, she said, pointing to her bedside table with magazines, and here is your bedroom, she added, showing us the walk-in closet, then crossing the narrow hallway, here is your bathroom-living room-patio" (114). This compression of space represents the shrinking freedoms allowed to Dominicans during Trujillo's reign and in the upheaval that followed. They suffer limited access to spaces, even in what might be called "private" spaces, because all space has become public space, subject to the ruler in such a political climate. Anita has only the bathroom window from which she has "a bird's-eye view of the grounds of the embassy. But unlike a bird, I can't fly free . . . except in my imagination" (109). Anita's imagination, manifest in her own writings, reflects Alvarez's narrative space as a safe place to inscribe the terrors they both experienced as young girls under dictatorship and revolution.

The walk-in closet in the Mancinis' home serves as a safe space for Anita and her mother, reminiscent of another closet that plays a significant role in both *How the García Girls Lost Their Accents* and *¡Yo!*, On the day the Garcías leave the Dominican Republic, they do so because of the arrival of the SIM—Trujillo's secret military police—to investigate an assassination plot against Trujillo. When they pull up to the house, Carlos García hides in a large walk-in closet with a back panel that leads to "a cubicle with a vent that opens out above the shower in the bathroom. Air and a little light. A couple of towels, a throw pillow, a sheet, a chamber pot, a container of filtered water, aspirin, sleeping pills, even a San Judas, patron of impossible causes" (196). As in *Before We Were Free*, only small and, more important, hidden spaces are safe in the period that Alvarez depicts in these novels. Another small, isolated place that Carlos García uses during the *trujillato* is his study. "It was a safe place to store anything," he remembers in *¡Yo!*, "because no one was allowed in my study, not even the maids" (299). Alvarez's insistence on the association between access to physical space and the freedom of intellect—in Anita's free imagination and in Carlos's study—emerges in her depictions of women's creativity and improvisation in the face of displacement and dissonance.

The most politicized of Alvarez's novels, *In the Time of the Butterflies* explores the spaces of the entire country under Trujillo's rule. The Mirabal sisters—Minerva, Dedé, Patria, and María Teresa—experience the same constraints on their freedom of movement and choice that the García girls describe. Minerva, in particular, longs to go away to school. She convinces her father to let her and two of her sisters attend school in the capital, "[a]nd that's how I got free. I don't mean just going to sleepaway school on a train with a trunkful of new things. I mean in my head after I got to Inmaculada and met Sinita and saw what happened to Lina and realized that I'd just left a small cage to go to a bigger one, the size of our whole country" (13). The country has become a cage, Minerva comes to understand, because it is under the absolute control of Trujillo, who makes no distinction between public and private spaces, between family and government property; in fact, "[t]he first thing Trujillo would do when someone's anti-regime activities were discovered was to go after the whole family" (*Something* 119), and "[i]f you were caught harboring any enemies of the regime even if you yourself were not involved in their schemes, you would be jailed and everything you owned would become the property of the government" (*In the Time* 165). When Minerva, Patria, and Mate are later accused of "anti-regime activities," Patria experiences these policies herself:

> They tore the house apart, hauling away the doors, windows, and the priceless mahogany beams of Pedrito's old family rancho. It was like watching her life dismantled before her very eyes, Patria said, weeping—the glories she had trained on a vine; the Virgencita in the silver frame blessed by the Bishop of Higüey; the wardrobe with little ducks she had stenciled on when Raulito was born. All of it violated, broken, desecrated, destroyed. Then they set fire to what was left. (192)

The space of Patria's home is also the space of her self—her experiences, her memories, her identity. As with her novels of exile, Alvarez again emphasizes in *In the Time of the Butterflies* the interrelationship between family, space, and the state.

At the same time that Minerva discovers that the whole country has become a cage under Trujillo's rule, she finds her school in the capital to be a place of personal freedom, specifically in regard to her intellect. She longs to remain and attend the university but instead must return to the family home. She laments, "Three years cooped up at home since I'd graduated from Inmaculada, and I was ready to scream with boredom. The worst part was getting newsy letters from Elsa and Sinita in the capital. They were taking a Theory of Errors class" (85). Minerva longs for the intellectual experience of the university as she finds that at home she is "cooped up" by traditional demands of women, which do not include attending college but instead center on marriage and childrearing. Moreover, Minerva does not initially see the home as a space of resistance or liberation.

It is Patria who fully comes to understand the space of the home as a powerful space of revolution. An oppositional space of political activism,

economic enterprise, and creative rebellion, the domestic space can coun-
teract the victimization of the Dominican people at the hands of Trujillo.
Patria is initially resistant to participating in the resistance movement with
Minerva and Mate because of the risks to Patria's own home and her husband's family land if their activities are discovered. She changes her mind
after attending a religious retreat in the mountains and witnessing what
she calls the martyrdom of forty-nine men and boys, murdered by "our
brainwashed *campesinos* who had hunted down their own liberators"
(164) during the Fourteenth of June uprising against Trujillo. At the
retreat, the women meet and eat "in a big airy room with a large picture
window. I sat with my back to the dazzling view so as not to be distracted
from His Word by His Creation" (160). As the rebels come down from the
mountains, however, and are attacked by their own countrymen, Patria
"saw a mess of glass and rubble on the floor, bodies huddled everywhere.
A wall had tumbled down and the tile floor was all torn up. Beyond,
through the jagged hole where the window had been, the closest moun-
tainside was a raging inferno" (161). After this tragedy, Patria understands
that even the Church is not a safe space, not a sanctuary from the violence
Trujillo has wrought on them all, and she opens first her property and
then her house to the underground movement, which names itself the
Fourteenth of June in honor of the martyrdom of those rebels.

Through Patria's gesture and her involvement in the group, Alvarez
emphasizes domestic space as an important site of resistance and struggle.[4] Patria's house becomes "the motherhouse" of the underground
(166), an image that connects the sacred institution of motherhood with
the space available for their efforts at liberation. It is also an image that
draws on Patria's personal experiences as a mother. She draws together
the space itself, her memories of that space, and the weapons required of
the revolution. The domestic space is not replaced by a political space;
rather, they both exist simultaneously in the home. She says:

> So it was that our house became the motherhouse of the move-
> ment. It was here with the doors locked and the front windows

shuttered that the ACC merged with the group Manolo had started over a year ago. [...] It was in this very parlor where Noris had begun receiving callers that the group gave themselves a name. [...] So it was between these walls hung with portraits, including El Jefe's, that the Fourteenth of June Movement was founded. [...] It was on this very Formica table where you could still see the egg stains from my family's breakfast that the bombs were made. [...] It was on this very bamboo couch where my Nelson had, as a tiny boy, played with the wooden guns his grandfather had made him that he sat now with Padre de Jesús, counting the ammunition for the .32 automatics we would receive in a few weeks in a prearranged spot. [...] It was on that very rocker where I had nursed every one of my babies that I saw my sister Minerva looking through the viewfinder of an M-1 carbine. [...] [I]t was in [Noris's] bedroom that we assembled the boxes. It was among her crocheted pink poodles and little perfume bottles and snapshots of her *quinceañera* party that we stashed our arsenal of assorted pistols and revolvers, three .38 caliber Smith and Wesson pistols, six .30 caliber M-1 carbines, four M-3 machine guns, and a .45 Thompson stole from a *guardia*. [...] It was on that very coffee table on which Noris had once knocked a tooth out tussling with her brother that the plans for the attack were drawn. [...] It was down this very hall and in and out of my children's bedrooms and past the parlor and through the back galleria to the yard that I walked those last days of 1959, worrying if I had done the right thing exposing my family to the SIM. I kept seeing that motherhouse up in the mountains, its roof caving in, its walls crumbling like a foolish house built on sand. (166–68)

Patria's remembered spaces coexist with the revolutionary activities, and the house takes on a multiplicity of functions even as it retains its physical form. Patria's house, however, is not merely a space; her memories, the stories she attaches to it, make of it a place—her home. Moreover, while the García girls find the paradox of remembered space to be a restriction on their womanhood in the Dominican Republic— a place they associate with the open spaces of the family compound and of the island's expansive beauty—Patria discovers that remembered space has multiple purposes. Similarly, she discovers that she does not have to forsake motherhood in order to be a resistance fighter; she can maintain both identities simultaneously, without sacrificing her commitment to either. This multiplicity is a hallmark of Alvarez's construction of womanhood, history, identity, narrative, genre, and creativity.

While Patria's revolutionary activities are focused on her home, Minerva and Mate are imprisoned for them, and their prison cell emerges as an important space in the novel. Alvarez not only describes the cell in detail, but she also provides a sketch of it in Mate's diary. As Mate writes, the cell consists of "[t]hree bolted steel walls, steel bars for a fourth wall, a cement floor. Twenty-four metal shelves ('bunks'), a set of twelve on each side, a bucket, a tiny washbasin under a small high window. [. . .] Twenty-four of us eat, sleep, write, go to school, and use the bucket—everything—in a room 25 by 20 of my size 6 feet" (228). The small space of the cell houses not only the daily routines of the life of the body, but it also houses the life of the mind. Small as it is, the cell is not too small for education, and Alvarez's specific reference to writing demonstrates her insistence on that act of creativity as a matter of survival in the same way the women must eat and sleep. In the cell, "[a]ll us politicals have our bunks on the east side, and so we've asked for the southeast corner to be 'ours.' Minerva says that except for closed meetings, anyone can join our classes and discussions, and many have" (228–29). Out of the small space of the cell, the politicals are claiming some space of their own, space that is transformed into a place—the southeast corner—for their activities. They define both the space and the purpose themselves, seeking some measure of autonomy in a prison environment. The confined space of the southeast corner paradoxically becomes the location of the larger purpose of revolution and freedom.

Perhaps the most significant space that Alvarez writes into her descriptions of the Dominican Republic is the patio in the family compound, which emerges as a liminal space of arrivals and departures, a gateway between multiple worlds. Alvarez begins *How the García Girls Lost Their Accents* in that space, as Yolanda remembers her childhood in that setting and suddenly longs for what she has not even realized she had been missing. First, the Dominican patio is functional in a way not possible in the northeastern United States. Second, the patio provides a view of the landscape, in contrast to the closed spaces that Alvarez constructs for the Garcías in New York. Third, the patio provides an in-between space—both inside and outside the house—that effects a multiplicity of function that winds throughout the whole of Alvarez's work. Its multiplicity of function does not, however, prevent the patio from being subject to Dominican traditions that dictate its composition. Yolanda observes, "The patio is sex-segregated—the men sit to one side, smoking their cigars and tinkling their rum drinks. The women lounge on wicker armchairs by the wall lamps, exclaiming over whatever there is to be exclaimed about" (126–27). With their exclamations, the patio also becomes a place where women create narrative. In this scene and in other scenes throughout Alvarez's writings, the patio is always a place to come together—as a family, as revolutionaries, as visitors, as lovers, even as spies. It is a space of multiplicity in both function and location, serving as the focus of Dominican life.

The paradox of remembered space lies in its multiplicity. Spaces are not merely open, undefined areas but rather are transformed into places through storytelling; physical and psychological spaces express multiple functions, activities, and identities and both space and place are transformed by memory into places that may never have existed, except in memory itself. Similarly, multiplicity is apparent in the various identities of the García girls who maintain ties to their homeland even in exile in the United States, and in the multiple identities of the Mirabal sisters who are daughters, wives, sisters, mothers, and revolutionary fighters. Alvarez draws these roles and activities together in the narrative space of her novels, and she refuses to sacrifice or obscure any of them in order to present some imagined unified vision of the U.S. Caribbean woman in the twentieth century. The multiplicity of identities for post-colonial writers can be maintained through such close descriptions of the spaces, places, and landscapes of their experience. As new maps of a continuing de-colonial struggle, these narratives reveal the significance of remembered spaces—they can be claimed out of colonial history and transformed into sites of resistance. ⌒

ASYMPTOSY, GENDER, AND EXILE

The experience of exile conditions all of Julia Alvarez's writings. Writers in exile, either chosen or forced, inscribe displacement in their texts. As a writer in and of exile, Alvarez insists on the multiplicity of the places of her own migrations within the narrative space of her writings. Czeslaw Milosz, another well-known exile whose work Alvarez frequently cites,[1] has observed that the homeland is privileged as the "center," particularly for writers. Exile, however, "displaces that center or rather creates two centers" (38). Although Milosz's description of a dual-centered exile disrupts monolithic, place-based constructions of identity, nationality, and language, his notion of two centers reinforces traditional dichotomies of place: here/there, home/abroad, native/foreign. Such dichotomies ignore, or at least obscure, the multiple migrations and places of exile. In contrast to those static dichotomies, Amy Kaminsky argues that "exile is not a single experience, either across populations or over time" (38). Alvarez's experience as an exile has indeed been multiple rather than singular, or even dual, and the myriad locations of Alvarez's writings reveal her commitment to an inclusive and multiple cartography. As she writes a new country on the map, she inscribes a mestizaje of exile through multiplicity in structure, point of view, and identity.

Historically, exiles have written two types of literature about the displacement of exile: exile as a romanticized journey of self-exploration and triumph and, more recently, exile as a painful negotiation of space, place, and identity. One significant example of the latter emerges in the writings of Edward Said, who sees exile as "the crippling sorrow of estrangement" ("Reflections" 137). In contrast to texts such as E. H. Carr's *The Romantic Exiles*, Said argues that exile is "a contemporary political punishment." In response to the glorification of such punishment, Said calls upon writers in exile to "map territories of experience beyond those mapped by the literature of exile itself." He argues that the traditional literature of exile obscures or lacks representations of those disempowered and disenfranchised by reasons and realities of nationality, gender, race, class, ability, sexuality, ethnicity, and religion, and as such neglects "the hopelessly large numbers, the compounded misery of 'undocumented' people suddenly lost, without a tellable history" (Said, "Reflections" 139).

Alvarez has said that she seeks to write just those untellable experiences evoked by Said within the narrative voices and structures of her novels. She frequently finds that these unvoiced plots and viewpoints have been lost to traditional mappings of exile because they do not conform to standard literary practices. These losses are particularly relevant for women writers "because we don't think of plot in the same way men do. We don't structure our lives the same way, don't think of them as having a certain trajectory, as moving toward a certain apex, or ourselves as on a solitary voyage" (Lyons and Oliver 132). Alvarez, in fact, constructs throughout her writings a gendered map of exile, one in which the trajectories are neither linear nor solitary. Alvarez's novels in particular reveal multiple trajectories, apexes, and voyages, each approaching one another without merging into hybridity. Alvarez tells the untellable history of those missing from the literature of exile by creating an asymptotic space in her writing to map these territories of experience. Asymptotic pairs, which approach each other but never meet, appear throughout Alvarez's writings as she demonstrates the forced distance between country and self. Reading the geography of women's experiences in exile, Jane Marcus suggests that "[d]isplacement and distance are obviously different for women who are already displaced by gender in their home cultures" (275). This double displacement contributes to women's inability to become "hybrid" in their new culture or to adapt to the conflicting expectations, demands, and roles readily assimilated into a new, "hybridized" identity.

Alvarez's own story exemplifies the problematic nature of hybridity and exile. Alvarez and her family arrived in the United States in 1960, near the end of the *trujillato*.[2] Her father was involved in the underground resistance movement to overthrow the dictator. When his activities in the movement were discovered, his "[f]riends in the States rigged up a fellowship for my father. The pretext was that he would study heart surgery there since there wasn't a heart surgeon in the Dominican Republic" (*Something* 16). He applied for a two-year visa for himself and for his family, and when their papers arrived, Alvarez began to realize that their "vacation" to the United States to "see snow" might be a very long sojourn after all. Living in the United States, Alvarez remembers the arrival of their visa documents and wonders "if those papers had set us free from everything we loved" (19). Such "freedom" underlies the political paradox of exile for the Alvarez family: "This great country that had offered my parents a refuge had also created the circumstances that made them have to seek refuge in the first place" (108). Although Alvarez stops short of indicting the U.S. government for its sometime support of Trujillo's dictatorship—and the concomitant oppression, terror, and violence that resulted—this indication of her awareness of that role reveals yet another conflict and apparent contradiction in her own experience of exile.[3] She recognizes that freedom is a concept contingent on displacement, political power, and national relationships that supercede individual interests in favor of the state.

Exile, for Alvarez, was "a loss" (*Something* 100), which she describes in the poem "Exile" as a loss "much larger than I understood" (*Other Side* 26). "Overnight," she writes, "we lost everything: homeland, an extended family, a culture" (*Something* 139). She remembers in the poem "Beginning Again" that while living in the United States, "[s]ometimes I wake up in the middle of the night/ counting over our losses again." These "losses, the wrong answers/ (some painfully lived out)" are "so deeply grieved in the heart-/ broken mind so that we cannot possibly recover" (*Other Side* 53). These losses forced her to reinvent herself, which "was part of the excitement as well as the confusing challenge of America" (*Something* 115). This confusing challenge should not necessarily be read as an antidote to or an assuagement of the losses of exile but rather as the creation of additional selves that constantly interact with the selves not lost to memory.

Alvarez's depiction of her own self-creation reveals that the hybridity often ascribed to identity in exile is an inadequate paradigm. Hybridity fails to render visible—to map, in a sense—the multiplicity of roles imposed on exiles in both the original and the adopted cultures. Alvarez's view of the Caribbean experience of exile reveals an accumulation of differences that never integrate to form a coherent whole, challenging monolithic notions of hybrid "culture" and hybrid "literature" in postcolonial societies. This failure to integrate—this dis-integration—suggests the mathematical concept of asymptotes—two lines that draw increasingly close but meet only in infinity, a space that does not exist. As part of the project to define and describe the narrative relationship between exile and womanhood, I argue that asymptosy characterizes Alvarez's work and provides a visual representation of the various components of Alvarez's writing.

This asymptotic approach to Alvarez's work differs from previous criticism of her novels, in which hybridity has been the dominant paradigm. In "New Ways of Telling," Jacqueline Stefanko argues that Alvarez, in *How the García Girls Lost Their Accents*, creates "hybrid texts in order to 'survive in diaspora'" (50), suggesting that "the intercultural questions of identity" in Alvarez's work evolve "from being 'in-between,' from the condition of hybridity" (67). This notion, however, is too reductive for Alvarez's work. What propels her novels is an accumulation of identities rather than the integration of identities into a single psychological whole. This accumulation thus exposes the dis-integration of identities experienced by Yolanda García in *How the García Girls Lost Their Accents* and *¡Yo!*; by Camila Henríquez and Salomé Ureña in *In the Name of Salomé*; and by Minerva Mirabal in *In the Time of the Butterflies*. Moreover, Alvarez complicates traditional constructions of exile as simply the consequence of physical displacement by exploring what might be seen as a psychological exile for Minerva and Salomé, exiles who never leave their countries. The gender roles they face at home, in exile, and in the artificial breach between their private and public lives reveal a concentration of differences that never converge but instead remain asymptotic, unassimilated identities.

ASYMPTOSY AND THE REMEMBERED HOMELAND

Alvarez reveals asymptosy to be characteristic of exile in her depictions of the Dominican Republic, the homeland of her characters. The memory of the island and the island itself never converge into a single geographical location or personal experience; home, for the exile, can never be recuperated because what exists in the memory of the exile never existed in reality at all. Rather, Alvarez's characters see the island "through the lens of loss" (*García Girls* 212). Returning to the Dominican Republic at the beginning of *How the García Girls Lost Their Accents*, Yolanda García feels nostalgia for the country of her birth, believing that she has "never felt at home in the States, never" (12). Yolanda, however, is not "at home" in the Dominican Republic, either. She speaks "halting Spanish" with an accent and struggles against the gendered expectations within her family; she wishes to travel, alone, by car throughout the island of her memory while her aunts insist that "[a] woman just doesn't travel alone in this country. Especially these days" (9). Unwilling to surrender the independence she enjoys in the United States, Yolanda is uncomfortable in the Dominican Republic.

Yolanda's asymptotic relationship with her imagined home and the real island reappears in *¡Yo!* In this novel, many of the characters from *How the García Girls Lost Their Accents* present their side of the story that Yolanda has purportedly told in the first novel. Outraged that Yolanda has used them as "fictional fodder" (3) and that their lives have been "worked over in print" (4), her "plagiarized" sisters, parents, cousins, aunts, lovers, and friends narrate their own lives as well as Yolanda's. Such a change in perspective presents an outside view of Yolanda's struggle to come to terms with the Dominican Republic of her imagination. Her Dominican relatives fear that the García girls have long viewed the island as "their summer-vacation homeland" (51). Yet, as in the first novel, Yo is seeking more than a tan when she visits the island, searching for the homeland of her memory. On one visit to the Dominican Republic, her lover Dexter pleads with her to "come on home," to which she replies, "'What do you mean, *home*,' she snaps. [. . .] 'This *is* my home'" (192). From Dexter's point of view in the United States, however, "[s]he hasn't lived there for a quarter of a century. She works here, makes love here, has her friends here, pays taxes here, will probably die here" (193). Dexter observes that "when she talks about the D.R., she gets all dewy-eyed as if she were crocheting a little sweater and booties for that island, as if she had given birth to it herself out of the womb of her memory" (193). Dexter echoes the traditional conflations of women with landscape and mother-hood with nation—apparent in images from colonial mappings of the island, to symbols of woman-as-nation during the French Revolution, to the concept of Republican motherhood in the United States.[4]

Traditional attempts to conflate homeland and motherhood also resonate in Alvarez's fourth novel, *In the Name of Salomé* (2000). This novel imagines the story of Salomé Ureña, *la poetisa nacional* of the Dominican Republic, and her daughter, Camila Henríquez. Alvarez writes that *In the Name of Salomé* "is not biography or historical portrai-ture or even a record of all I learned, but a work of the imagination." As fictional characters, Salomé and Camila "are based on historical figures, but they are recreated in the light of questions that we can only answer, as they did, with their own lives: Who are we as a people? What is a patria? How do we serve? Is love stronger than anything else in the world?" Alvarez seeks to "understand the great silence from which these two women emerged and into which they have disappeared, leaving us to dream up their stories and take up the burden of their songs" (357). Camila has disappeared into the silence of exile, disconnected from her *patria* and her mother. After losing her mother and her homeland at age three, Camila has spent her life in search of both. In all her wander-ing, "[e]very decade a new address" (334), Camila realizes, "It is my mother I am looking for" (242). The home she has constructed in her mind is what we might call a *matria*—not a patria—a mother/land in the territory of her memory. Her mother and *la patria*—whose destinies are linked from the first line of Salomé's own life story—are entwined in Camila's mind in such a way that she cannot separate them, having spent her life in search of each, or both. As with her homeland, Camila writes of her mother, "I learned to be with her as an absence all my life" (337).

The exile, however, can never return home, as Alvarez demonstrates in Camila's search for her mother and for her idea of the Dominican Republic. This permanent displacement, which Camila's brother Pedro calls "the terrible moral disinheritance of exile" (112), creates for Camila a life embodied by her own analogy, "house is to home as country is to blank" (343). Unlike a house, home is tied to notions of family, memory, and belonging; Camila has never been able to forge analogous ties to her country—nor really even to identify it—because of the multiple displacements of her life. Camila's exile causes her to feel as though she has missed "all the important things she was promised that have not yet happened: a great love, a settled home, a free country" (79). The "island at the center" of Camila's search "is as impossible to reach as the hypothetical Antillas that reappeared time and again, always fleetingly, on the cosmographers' charts" (Benítez-Rojo 4). Because Camila has lived her life in exile, she has no idea what the Dominican Republic is, and the creation of it in her mind does not fit the reality. She can, therefore, never go home or reach the island of her imagination. That is actually the terrible moral disinheritance of exile.

ASYMPTOTIC NARRATIVE STRUCTURE AND POINT OF VIEW

In her fictional inscription of Camila's and Salomé's lives, Alvarez creates an asymptotic narrative, twisting and circling Camila's life around her mother's story. The trajectory of Camila's life in exile gradually and increasingly approaches her mother's history, as well as her homeland, but their lives remain separate, never quite connecting. Camila, the exile, circles the source—her mother, her patria—but the circle of her own narrative also demonstrates that the conflicting experiences that mark her life—womanhood and patriarchy, exile and return—cannot converge. Predicated on Camila's inability to recuperate what is lost in exile, the asymptotic structure of the narrative mirrors the asymptotic distance created by the loss of homeland, family, and culture.

The structure of Alvarez's novels resembles a helix, twisting the Dominican Republic and the United States together, binding the stories of these women's lives. This form creates what Julia Barak has called "a narrative spiral," a reflection of Benítez-Rojo's "visual explanation, a graphic picture of what the Caribbean is," analogous to "the spiral chaos of the Milky Way" (4). Throughout *In the Name of Salomé*, Salomé's story is told chronologically, from 1850 to 1894, in chapters that span several years, bridging the time between the major events of her life—childhood, coming of age, national recognition, courtship, marriage, motherhood, and terminal illness. In contrast, Camila's life, told in alternating chapters, moves backward in time from 1960 to 1897, each chapter devoted primarily to a specific event and location, leaving great gaps in time and space. The asymptotic spiral created by the two stories renders visible the exile's inability to return home. Salomé's story ends just as Camila is about to enter the world after Salomé's difficult labor. In the final chapter of Camila's story, however, she is three years old, aboard a ship leaving Santo Domingo after her mother's death. As asymptotes, mother and child never meet in the novel because the three years they shared in this life are not included. Alvarez instead imagines the disjunction of their experience—lives lived apart but connected by family and country.

Alvarez similarly structures her other novels, creating a spiral in time and place, an asymptotic conception of the spaces women inhabit in exile. In *How the García Girls Lost Their Accents*, the "narrative spiral" of the text begins in the present with Yolanda's return to the Dominican Republic and moves backward in time. The fifteen chapters are divided into five sections, the first spanning seventeen years while the second and third are temporally compact, centering on the circumstances immediately following the family's flight from the Dominican Republic and on a description of their lives on the island prior to exile, respectively. In the final chapter of the novel, "The Drum," Yolanda as a child, five years before she will be forced to leave the island, begins to understand something about home and family when she tries to take a kitten from its mother and keep it for a pet. A passing stranger tells her that "[t]o take it away would be a violation of its natural right to live" (*García Girls* 285), but Yolanda takes it anyway. The cat haunts her dreams. At this point in the novel, time stops moving backward and begins moving forward, allowing Alvarez to "collaps[e] all time now so that it fits in what's left of my story" (289). The cat "lurk[s] in the corners of my life, her magenta mouth opening, wailing over some violation that lies at the center of my art" (290). The cat reminds Yolanda that what lie at the center of her art are family, exile, and voice.

In addition to the time-space structures of her novels, Alvarez employs a multiplicity of viewpoints, which also evince the asymptotic world of exile. In *How the García Girls Lost Their Accents*, Alvarez employs both first-person and third-person points of view, allowing each of "the Four Girls," as well as Mami and Papi, to narrate the individual chapters. Ellen McCracken argues in *New Latina Narrative* that these "implicitly autobiographical first- and third-person narrators [serve] to depict the opposing positions of identity that the members of one family enter into in the move between two national realities" (192). These opposing positions of identity create for individual women the dis-integration of exile. The moniker of "the Four Girls" threatens to meld them into a single identity, which Alvarez rejects by giving each García girl—Carla, Sandi, Yolanda, and Fifi—their own narrative point of view in the novel.

Alvarez's continual change of narrative points of view also disrupts traditional narrative structures and commits "formal and diegetic transgressions" (McCracken 28). The first four chapters of *How the García Girls Lost Their Accents* are written in third-person, character-specific narrative, but the fifth chapter is narrated in the first-person by Yolanda. In the second section of the novel, which takes place just after the Garcías arrive in the United States, three chapters are recounted in the third-person and one, again from Yolanda, is presented in the first person. The first chapter of this section, however, is narrated in the first-person plural, ostensibly from the point of view of all four of the García girls. The voice of all four girls "functions implicitly as a metanarrative of the storytelling process in the collection as a whole" (McCracken 29) in which the multiplicity of viewpoints enacts the various identities these girls face in exile. While their individual voices maintain separate identities, the chapters told through their collective voice remind readers of the similar processes they face as Dominican females in the United States. Alvarez inscribes their unique responses while she both claims and values the family connection and the solidarity of female communities.

Although her conception of hybridity proves inadequate to describe the García girls and Alvarez herself, Stefanko's connection between movement and narration neatly illustrates the link between Alvarez's narrative "transgressions" and exile. Stefanko first suggests that "[d]ue to the shifting, unstable terrain they inhabit, Latin American (migrant) women writers question and reject the assumption that a unitary, synthesizing narrator is capable of telling the stories they have to disclose, instead opting for a narrative stance that includes multiple voicings" (51). These multiple voicings, she argues, are related to the migrations they experience, points of view that reveal "their external and internal dialogues, suggesting that utilizing the multiple voices is a manifestation of the subject of consciousness-shifting among multiple positions" (52). The multiple narrators come together within the narrative space of the novel and begin Alvarez's project of mapping the multiple geographics of identity.

In the final section of *How the García Girls Lost Their Accents*, four of the five chapters are written in the first person, and only the story of the circumstances surrounding the Garcías' flight from the Dominican Republic, "Blood of the Conquistadores," is told from the third-person point of view, focused on all six members of the family. These perspectives, McCracken suggests, provide "competing versions of events for readers to compile" (28) and thus refute the existence of a single History or even a single Truth. As the girls move closer in time and space to their island home, they increasingly tell their own memories, but the inability for the Garcías to assimilate fully into society in the United

States, or for the García women in particular to integrate the multiple identities that they face, resonates in the lingering third-person sequences in the novel. Without these third-person sequences, which are themselves part of Alvarez's multiple perspectives, the map of the Garcias' exile would fail to reveal the people and forces they affect and by which they are affected during their multiple exiles and returns.

Taking up the story of the García family in ¡Yo!, Alvarez again mixes third- and first-person viewpoints as Yo's friends and family tell the stories of their lives with Yolanda. Such a mixture of viewpoints and narrators allows Alvarez to demonstrate the instability and uncertainty not only of Yo's life in exile but of fiction and life in general. These viewpoints present an asymptotic spiral, each drawing closer and closer to Yolanda, the fixed point of their multiple stories. This spiral stems from Alvarez's desire to rewrite traditional stories of exile, in particular the artist-in-exile-as-hero story, which she describes in an interview with Bridget Kevane and Juanita Heredia:

> ¡Yo! is very much a "portrait of the artist." Again, this type of literature follows a very canonical structure: the artist as the aristocrat of spirit is always awarded the point of view. Western literature gives the top position to the artist, especially with romanticism, Wordsworth, and later Joyce and Proust. Well, I've never been interested in hierarchies. (26)

The structure and narrative viewpoints of ¡Yo! undermine not only hierarchies of exclusion by giving at least sixteen people a voice but also hierarchies of the literary canon, for Alvarez considers Yolanda herself an artist equal to Joyce's Stephen Dedalus and Proust's Marcel.

Alvarez also employs a variety of narrative viewpoints in In the Time of the Butterflies, the story of the Mirabal sisters, who are both members and symbols of the underground resistance movement. These sisters, described by McCracken as "important female political icons," allow Alvarez to reread and, I would add, rewrite the Dominican Republic's political history, thus insisting "that the U.S. mainstream come to terms not only with recent Dominican history but with non-official versions of that history" (McCracken 84). This novel allows Alvarez to write the "untellable history" of women's experiences during the trujillato, experiences not merely domestic but also political, demonstrating the multiple identities of these Dominican heroines.

Alvarez uses asymptotic points of view to map those competing identities. The surviving Mirabal sister, Dedé, provides the focus for the beginning of each section in 1994 and then recalls events leading up to her sisters' assassination in 1960. Dedé's viewpoint is complicated by the character of the *gringa dominicana*, a double for Julia Alvarez herself, who interviews Dedé while researching the Mirabal sisters. Dedé's first-person narratives are thus presented "as told to" the gringa, and this strategy extends to the stories of Minerva, María Teresa, and Patria, each of whom narrates a chapter in the three sections of the book, spanning the years between 1938 and November 25, 1960, when they were assassinated by Trujillo's secret police on a deserted mountain road. In the narratives of all four sisters, the time of the action never overlaps; they are each responsible for a different time segment of their life stories. The different narrative points of view combined with the strict temporal borders between the chapters serve to create some distance among the girls, resisting the imposition of a hybridity that could conflate the individual personalities of the four sisters into one monolithic identity, heroines of the Dominican Republic. While Gus Puleo argues that the different narrative voices and perspectives work as a strategy that "suggests the collective identity of Dominicans" (11), such a collective identity exists simultaneously with Alvarez's desire to portray these women as individuals. By telling the story from their individual points of view, Alvarez reinstates their individuality and creates an asymptotic space between them that resists a hybridized view of their role in Dominican history.

The asymptotic spaces among the Mirabal sisters are also apparent between Camila and her mother in the different points of view Alvarez employs in *In the Name of Salomé*. Camila recounts her mother's story because, as she tells her friend Marion, it is also her own story; oddly, then, Salomé's story is presented in the first person and Camila's in the third person. Camila, in a sense, deploys the autobiographical "I" in Salomé's story, which she is ostensibly telling to Marion, while the very story to which Camila has access—her own—is told in the third person. Through this third-person point of view, Camila is able to indulge in "the habit of erasing herself, of turning herself into the third person, a minor character, the best friend (or daughter!) of the dying first-person hero or heroine. Her mission in life—after the curtain falls—is to tell the story of the great ones who have passed on" (8). Camila never considers herself one of "the great ones" but merely "a daughter," two identities that cannot converge in the self she has constructed in light of socially accepted roles for women, which is, ironically, the single and unified voice of hegemony. The polyphony of Alvarez's narrators allow her to achieve what Bakhtin has called "novelness," which is dialogic in nature and, as Julian Holloway and James Kneale interpret it, "characterized by the articulation of many voices that remain unmerged" (77).[5] In Alvarez's work, these unmerged voices articulate asymptosy as a gendered expression of the experience of exile.

ASYMPTOSY, GENDER, AND EXILE

The gendered dimension of exile emerges in Alvarez's construction of asymptotic relationships and identities for her women characters, experiences that reveal the dis-integration of women's lives. Alvarez herself recognized at a young age the contradictions of the gendered expectations and roles for women in exile. Although women in many cultures are faced with conflicting expectations, the multiple places of exile result in both an increased number of cultures with their varying expectations and an increased desire to assimilate and relieve the psychic discomfort of displacement. As a young girl in the Dominican Republic, Alvarez realized that it was "the boy cousins who are asked what they want to do with their lives. Girls are told we are going to be wives and mothers. If we're asked at all, it's usually how many children we want and whom we might marry"

(*Something* 135). Underlying Dominican customs Alvarez recognizes the "basic assumption that as a female you gave yourself to your familia." As a writer, however, "I especially found my vocation at odds with my training as a female and as a member of la familia" (122). As a struggling writer, Alvarez married twice, and each time, "I put aside my writing. Back in those pre-women's movement days, wives were wives, first and foremost" (142). She wonders whether, if she and her sisters "had been sons, it would have been easier for our parents to allow us the independence we needed in order to survive in this new country" (122). These conflicting roles of woman, wife, and writer approach one another but never merge, providing her with a multiplicity of identities that permits her to conceive the polyphonic voices of her novels. The independence that she had seen as possible for middle-class, straight, white women in the 1970s appears to conflict with her perception of Dominican mandates of motherhood.

In order to understand better for herself these contradictions, Alvarez writes about the Dominican ideology of womanhood, arguing that "[a] woman did not have a public voice. She did not have a public life" (*Something* 122). This imagined public/private distinction points to class privilege; women of the working classes have traditionally found their private lives made public through work.[6] When Alvarez's middle-class women characters find a collision—not a compound—of the various roles they play, Alvarez demonstrates the artificiality of the public/private split for women of all classes. That Minerva, Camila, and Salomé occupy political space with their activism and that Salomé, Camila, and Yolanda occupy public space through their writings demonstrate Alvarez's construction of narrative space as a female space in her novels, a space in which both fictional and historical characters negotiate the conflicting demands of creativity and womanhood.

Asymptosy is emblematic of a variety of those conflicting demands in Salomé's life in *In the Name of Salomé*: her relationship to her country, her identities as poet and woman, and the reconstruction of her legend after her death. From these relationships Alvarez creates a coil of asymptotic lives, tightly binding but never blending the competing identities of

Camila, her mother, and their homeland in various combinations. Salomé's narrative begins with these words: "The story of my life starts with the story of my country" (13), immediately charting a parallel course for the development of both Salomé and the Dominican Republic. To ensure that readers are familiar with the Dominican Republic's unstable identity—"thirty-one [wars] just in [Salomé's] lifetime" (110)—Alvarez introduces the volatility both in Salomé's own life and in the country's history. Born six years after the Dominican Republic declared its independence from Haiti in 1844, Salomé comes of age with her country, both experiencing crises of hope, independence, and identity.

Salomé dreams of being a poet, a dream that is also linked to her country. She longs to "free la patria with my sharp quill and bottle of ink" (50). Using the pseudonym Herminia to protect herself from the ever-changing governments, Salomé writes poetry that is "waking up the body politic." Herminia, Salomé writes, is "going to bring down the regime with pen and paper" (62). Situating herself within the Dominican tradition linking poetry and politics—another asymptotic relationship—Salomé sees her verses as powerful and liberatory. When the Dominican Republic becomes a colony of Spain again during the years between 1861 and 1865, "[i]t was a time for poetry, even if it was not a time for liberty," largely because "[i]n the days of being a colony again, the newspapers were full of poetry. The Spanish censor let anything with rhymed lines pass, and so every patriot turned into a poet" (55). When Buenaventura Báez takes power, he begins to exile poets "for writing poems against the new regime." Salomé notes that with Báez's rule, the Dominican Republic "had left off being a colony to become a dictatorship with a censor who understood the power of poetry" (60).

In addition to political power, Salomé discovers that her poetry also has the power to attract admirers. One of Salomé's first suitors, Federico Henríquez, calls on Salomé, but, she writes, "[h]e was seeing the famous poetisa. [. . .] He was not seeing me, Salomé, of the funny nose and big ears with hunger in her eyes and Africa in her skin and hair" (94). For Federico and the rest of the Dominican people, Salomé writes, "[i]t's as if I had on a disguise, a famous face" (87). That famous face—a public face—conflicts with the picture she has of herself. She feels pressure, however, to disguise her private face for fear of disappointing her burgeoning patria. When that relationship falters, Federico's brother, Pancho, calls on "Salomé Ureña, la musa de la patria" (134). Salomé realizes that if she wants Pancho, "all [she] has to do is keep writing" (135). Her sister, Ramona, warns her, "Pancho's in love with your poetry, not with you. Even if he mistakes the two, you should not" (132), yet another asymptotic allusion. Salomé herself laments that people "don't love me, Ramona. They love la poetisa" (92). Despite Pancho's illusions and Salomé's disillusionment, they ultimately marry. He calls her "¡Mi musa, mi esposa, mi amor, mi tierra!" (270), conflating Salomé, her poetry, and the Dominican Republic into a single woman who does not want to bear so many identities. The putative conflation of Salomé, her poetry, and her patria is highly gendered in this novel as it draws on the constructs of woman-as-muse, woman-as-landscape, and woman-as-helpmeet— merely an extension or reflection of her husband's activities and accomplishments. Alvarez deploys asymptosy to reject this conflation and to demonstrate the difficulty for women writers of the nineteenth century to integrate their lives with their careers.

Salomé's role as *la poetisa nacional* is also gendered from the beginning. Salomé is a member "of the fair sex" (131), which shapes the perceptions of others and her perception of herself as a poet and a woman. Salomé writes, "I had been raised in a country where national heroines tied their skirts down as they were about to be executed. I did not know it was possible for a woman to reach over and touch a man's arm of her own accord" (139), revealing the contradiction between the political and the sexual freedom allowed to the national poet. At a reading of her poetry, someone applauds her and praises her by saying, "What a man that woman is," a remark that, Salomé observes wryly, "was meant to be a compliment, I suppose" (141). About her abilities as a poet, she dismisses the "rumors that I heard voices or that the angel Gabriel came to me in dreams" (91), rumors that reflect people's doubts about the fair sex's ability to produce exceptional writing and the possibility of their ever viewing her various "faces" as one. Moreover, being *la musa* is not precisely the same as being *la poetisa;* the muse, while an inspiration to others, has been traditionally conceived as a woman to be exalted, coaxed, and tempted. Once reached, the muse confers her favors, a highly sexualized process of objectification. Salomé as *la musa de la patria* finds only dis-integration, the impossibility of integrating the role of poetisa with that of wife, mother, and muse. Although the two draw increasingly close together, they never integrate into a single, complete, meaningful psychological identity.

Salomé finds perhaps most painful the disconnection between her body and intellect as the image of la musa de la patria is constructed for her by her readers. As a result of her fame as a poet, Salomé experiences more deeply the desexualization that accompanied middle-class nineteenth-century womanhood. She writes "Quejas," a poem about women's desire that "released the woman inside me and let her free on paper" (143). When Ramona reads it, she tells Salomé, "You can't publish this. You're la musa de la patria. [. . .] Nobody thinks you have a real body" (144). For the readers of her work, these two constructs cannot occupy the same physical space. When Salomé writes a personal poem to her husband, he responds by exhorting her patriotic work: "You must think of your future as the bard of our nation," dismissing her *poemas intimos* in favor of the political power she can exercise. She responds, "I am a woman as well as a poet" (177), foregrounding the gendered conflict between her public role of poet and her private identity as a woman. This conflict could not be resolved for many nineteenth-century women writers,[7] and it is never resolved for Salomé. Her identities as la poetisa and as a woman—with desires and a body—never converge but in their dis-integration remain a source of discord and pain for her.

Salomé suffers for this dis-integration and her conflicting obligations: "I felt my first duty—after my wifely duties, of course—was to my writing" (177). Pancho exhorts his wife to her writing duties while unquestioningly expecting the wifely duties. That the "wifely duties" come first, "of course," underscores the hierarchy of her identities in Dominican society. Even Pancho seems to recognize that she cannot, in fact, be both wife/mother and poet, lamenting, "Had it not been for me and your children, you would have continued on that immortal path" to being the bard of la patria, to which Salomé responds, "'Ay, Pancho,' I said, shaking my head. 'My children are the only immortality I want'" (268). She has to remind him repeatedly that she is a woman before she is a poet. In doing so, she embraces the Dominican tradition that expects that women be only wives and mothers.

Salomé's adherence to traditional Dominican gender roles may spring from her own desire to alleviate the stress that dis-integration so obviously causes her. Behaving according to public expectations could heal her of what Sandra Gilbert and Susan Gubar have called the "dis-ease" of the nineteenth-century woman writer. What makes Salomé's dis-ease unique are the public expectations of her as a writer, one on whom the people feel the independence of their nation rests. Salomé the icon bears the weight of the de-colonial struggles for independence that various countries in the Caribbean fought during the nineteenth century. Aware of this weight, Salomé writes to Pancho, who is studying in Paris, that "I know you are still harboring the hope that—as you said the night before you left—I will 'create something of lasting value for the generations to come.' I have, Pancho: our three sons!" (213). Salomé has to choose specifically and deliberately to be a wife, a mother, and a woman who is herself and also a poet. This forced choice prevents her from achieving her full potential as a human being.

Even after Salomé's death, the various strands of her life remain dis-integrated. She is re-membered after her death by "[e]veryone in the family" because everyone had "touched up the legend" of Salomé (44). Pancho commissions a portrait of Salomé to commemorate la musa de la patria. This portrait exposes the racial component of her re-creation because it reflects Pancho's "whitened" Salomé as la poetisa nacional. Describing the portrait years later to a student helper, Camila says, "'Actually that pretty lady is my father's creation. [. . .] He wanted my mother to look like the legend he was creating,' Camila adds. 'He wanted her to be prettier, whiter'" (44). This whitened version of her mother is indeed only a legend; in fact, "[a]ccording to Mon, Salomé was a plain mulatto woman. In the posthumous portrait her father commissioned, Salomé is pale, pretty, with a black neck band and a full rosebud mouth, a beautifying and whitening of the Great Salomé, another one of her father's campaigns" (204–5). In a speech at the Mexican Fine Arts Center Museum, Alvarez showed three different portraits of Salomé Ureña. The first was a personal family portrait showing a dark-skinned woman, and the third, the "official" and "historical" portrait of la poetisa, reveals a white woman—with a fair complexion—with more delicate features. The difference between the way Pancho wants Salomé to be remembered and her actual existence reflects another dimension of the nature of asymptotes: their dynamism. Asymptotes—lines or spirals or curves—evoke movement and action, reflected explicitly by this evolving reinvention of the legend of la poetisa.

Also asymptotic, Camila's own life story is full of gaps in time and space, reflecting the Caribbean's resistance to "being captured by the cycles of the clock or calendar" (Benítez-Rojo 11). Alvarez's approach to Camila's story evinces the condition of exile, in which traveling makes Camila feel "like a heroine, suspended between lives, suspended between destinations" (107). Carolyn Heilbrun borrows a term from anthropology, liminality,[8] which she sees as being "poised upon uncertain ground, to be leaving one condition or country or self and entering upon another" (3). Liminality, as we see in Alvarez's rendering of Camila's life, is the paramount determinant of exile. Unable to return to the Dominican Republic, Camila's search for her own identity reveals "the most salient aspect of liminality [as] its unsteadiness, its lack of clarity about exactly where one belongs and what one should be doing, or wants to be doing" (Heilbrun 3). What Camila is doing, upon her retirement from Vassar at age sixty-six, is going through her mother's papers, discovering in the process the identity of her mother, her country, and herself, three asymptotic pairs that characterize Camila's life in exile.

Camila's task is "to sort out what to give the archives and what to destroy" (38). This task, according to Alvarez, is itself gendered because, in the Dominican Republic, "[i]t's a woman's place to be the guardian of the home and the family secrets, to keep things entre familia, to uphold the family honor" (*Something* 122). Camila has long defined herself by her family, her place in it, and her family members' roles in the government and development of the Dominican Republic. Chiding Camila for talking only about her family, Marion says, "I thought you were finally going to talk about yourself, Camila." Camila responds, "I *am* talking about myself" (*In the Name* 8). This connection to her family is belied by her own feeling that, "childless and motherless, she is a bead unstrung from the necklace of generations" of her family (2). Her father had been president, her brother Max has a job in the government, and, most important, her brother Pedro is "the one who received mother's legacy" (122) of poetry. That Camila defines herself by her family contradicts her sense that she does not really belong to their "necklace of the generations," that she is "the nobody among them" (38). Camila's asymptotic relationship with the men in her family reveals the dis-integration of her life.

Alvarez uses Camila's name to demonstrate the notion of the accumulation—rather than the integration—of Camila's identity and search for her mother/land. Camila likes to quote Emily Dickinson, to whom she compares her mother, saying, "I'm nobody—Who are you?" (3), but Camila is not nobody. Named for Salomé and "the wandering Camila" of a children's book, Camila uses her middle name alone throughout most of the book, going so far as to drop her first name from official records because she considers "it an honor she has not earned" (37). There are two notable exceptions. At the end of the novel, the beginning of Salomé's life, three-year-old Camila is hiding on a ship carrying her away from her home and the memory of her mother. Her family calls her repeatedly: "Salomé Camila! Salomé Camila!" and Camila thinks, "Salomé Camila, her mother's name and her name, always together. [. . .] She calls out, 'Here we are!'" (331). The second instance appears in the Epilogue, when Camila has finally returned to Santo Domingo. Selecting the marker for her grave, she insists that the stone read "Salomé Camila."

Alvarez uses these two occasions to draw together the two names, side by side, without merging them into one. Camila never uses her first name alone, but she wants to use both names to mark her "first permanent home" (334). To discover her mother, to draw Salomé next to her, Camila writes, "I learned her story. I put it side by side with my own. I wove our two lives together as strong as a rope and with it I pulled myself out of the pit of depression and self-doubt" (335). This twisting together of parallel stories, and thus identities, is accumulation without integration, the asymptotic experience of exile.

In her historical reconstruction of the Mirabal sisters, Alvarez similarly demonstrates the ways that alienation from la patria—its ideals and identity—results in a dis-integration of women's lives similar to that experienced in the physical displacement from the homeland. Minerva Mirabal is psychologically and socially alienated from her patria, a kind of internal exile. Although she never leaves the Dominican Republic, Minerva, as Alvarez portrays her in the novel, experiences both the loss of exile and an inability to reconcile the reality of her homeland with the country she imagines in her mind. Minerva's hopes for her country lead her to work in the underground Fourteenth of June Movement, a resistance network plotting Trujillo's assassination and liberation for Dominicans and the Dominican Republic.

Both a leader in and a symbol of the underground movement, Minerva finds dissonance between her political role as heroine and her personal role as wife and mother. When Minerva is imprisoned for her political activities, she becomes "the secret heroine of the whole nation" (*In the Time* 198), a role that she finds difficult to bear. Upon her release from prison, she discovers that "[m]y months in prison had elevated me to superhuman status" (259). Being a superhuman secret heroine, however, does not allow room for Minerva to be the wife and mother she also longs to be. In prison, Minerva wishes not for political meetings or plans to accumulate weapons; she mourns the minutes she must spend away from her children and yearns to play with them, care for them, dress them, and teach them. Minerva, however, discovers that as a political heroine she "does not belong to herself alone. She belongs to Quisqueya" (238), the original name of the Dominican Republic used by the resistance movement, an anticolonialist construction of the nation. Alvarez reveals the dissonance that Minerva finds between her roles as heroine and as wife/mother in Minerva's connection between space and identity. "All my life," Minerva says, "I had been trying to get out of the house. [. . .] First I wanted to go to boarding school, then university. When Manolo and I started the underground, I traveled back and forth from Monte Cristi to Salcedo, connecting cell with cell. I couldn't stand the idea of being locked up in any one life" (257). The physical spaces to which she has sought access reflect the lives she desired before her imprisonment. Minerva finds that those spaces and those lives belong to Minerva the *mariposa* and not to Minerva the woman. After she is released from prison "and put under house arrest, you'd have thought I was getting just the punishment for me. But to tell the truth, it was as if I'd been served my sentence on a silver platter. By then, I couldn't think of anything I wanted more than to stay home with my sisters at Mamá's, raising our children" (257). Her desire to embrace the role of mother suggests the psychological stress of symbolizing the hopes of an entire nation, all of whom, Dedé observes, have "romanticized [the family's] terror" (199).

Not belonging to herself alone, Minerva feels an obligation to her country as well as to her children and family, and her time in prison forces her to realize that surviving as her children's mother is more important than her role as political activist. After her release, she recognizes "[h]ow much it took to put on the hardest of all performances, being my old self again" (259). She finds herself leading a "double life," particularly for her imprisoned husband, in which "[o]utwardly, I was still his calm, courageous compañera. Inside the woman had got the upper hand" (267). Years later, Dedé recognizes the dissonance Minerva faced, worrying "that she has not kept enough from the children. But she wants them to know the living breathing women their mothers were. They get enough of the heroines from everyone else" (64). Alvarez herself warns her readers against making myths of these individual women because we can lose the meaning of their lives and deaths by "dismissing the challenge of their courage as impossible for us, ordinary men and women" (324). Alvarez sees their lives not only as instructional for the Dominican past but also as inspirational for its future. In the novel, Minerva's courage stems precisely from her life as an ordinary woman and citizen of the Dominican Republic. Her life becomes extraordinary in her ability to negotiate her multiple identities, which, while painful, are also empowering. Drawing strength and purpose from her roles as daughter, sister, wife, and mother, Minerva extends the confining space assigned to women through her work with the Fourteenth of June Movement. As with her identities, the spaces of her life multiply to offer her the leeway essential to her assertions of self.

The spaces of Yolanda García's life include both the United States and the Dominican Republic, locations that evince geographically the asymptotic dis-integration of exile. Throughout *How the García Girls Lost Their Accents* and *¡Yo!*, Alvarez presents the conflict from both masculine and feminine perspectives as well as the dominant cultural expectations of both within the United States and the Dominican Republic. Although living in New York, Yolanda's father maintains Dominican expectations of womanhood. Alvarez also reveals Dominican womanhood as constructed from outside the culture through the point of view of Victor Hubbard, who is attached to the American Embassy and is probably a CIA agent. During the long hours he spends with underage prostitutes, he comes to believe that "[t]hese Latin women, even when the bullets are flying and the bombs are falling, they want to make sure you have a full stomach, your shirt is ironed, your handkerchief is fresh. It's what makes the nice girls from polite society great hostesses, and the girls at Tatica's [brothel] such obliging lovers" (*García Girls* 207). Hubbard's conflation of all "Latin" women into a single category reflects the gendered construction of the feminine ideal. Victor Hubbard refuses to see the individuality of Dominican women, and he also presents an idealized, sexualized view of these women's domesticity, a misapprehension that will follow Alvarez's Dominican women into exile in the United States.

In the United States, Carlos García expects his daughters to conform to the domestic ideal that Victor Hubbard describes, but an ideal that demands the domesticity and dedication to men and the simultaneous suppression of women's sexuality (with the exception of prostitutes). Papi watches his girls carefully, monitoring their activities, limiting their opportunities, and warning them repeatedly about their behavior. One typical speech begins, "I don't want any loose women in the family," a warning "delivered communally, for even though there was usually the offending daughter of the moment, every woman's character could use extra scolding" (*Garcia Girls* 28). For Papi the possible performances of gender in the United States are as limited as they are in the Dominican Republic. Because "too much education might spoil [them] for marriage" (228), Papi compensates for their American education by sending them to the Island every summer. Because Papi views marriage as the paramount experience for women, the "hidden agenda" for these summer trips "was marriage to homeland boys, since everyone knew that once a girl married an American, those grandbabies came out jabbering in English and thinking of the Island as a place to go to get a suntan" (109). Unfortunately, Alvarez writes, "[h]is daughters had had to put up with this kind of attitude in an unsympathetic era. They grew up in the late sixties. Those were the days when wearing jeans and hoop earrings, smoking a little dope, and sleeping with their classmates were considered political acts against the military-industrial complex" (28).

Yolanda feels acutely the dis-integration of these contradictory expectations of exile in college, when she begins to have relationships with men. Yolanda writes, "I cursed my immigrant origins. If only I had been born in Connecticut or Virginia, I too would understand the jokes everyone was making on the last two digits of the year, 1969; I too would be having sex and smoking dope" (*García Girls* 94–95). She knows that her ethnic identity, her "immigrant origins," will clash with the identity she would prefer to construct in the United States: "I saw what a cold, lonely life awaited me in this country. I would never find someone who would understand my peculiar mix of Catholicism and agnosticism,

Hispanic and American styles" (99). When Yolanda dates her first boyfriend in college, Rudy Elmenhurst, his parents believe that it "should be interesting to find out about people from other cultures," which makes Yolanda feel "like a geography lesson for their son" (98). While Rudy is not interested in her lessons in geography, he does attempt to further her sexual education, spending his time and energy trying to convince her to go to bed with him. When she repeatedly refuses, he tells her "I thought you'd be all hot-blooded, being Spanish and all, and that under all that Catholic bullshit, you'd be really free, instead of all hung up like these cotillion chicks from prep schools" (99). Rudy's words are doubly hurtful; his conflation of her homeland with her language reveals a complete insensitivity to her identity as a person—a Dominican American person—and his derogatory reference to "cotillion chicks" demonstrates to Yolanda that her wish to have been born in Connecticut or Virginia—like the very women Rudy is disparaging—would still prevent her from the psychological wholeness—as a woman, as a citizen, as a writer—that she yearns to achieve.

Yolanda's later experiences with men reveal the same failure in their eyes and, thus, in her own. Her husband, John, makes a pro/con list about Yolanda, listing in the "for" column "*intelligent*" but on the opposite side of the page, "against: *too much for her own good*" (*García Girls* 74). This dual interpretation of one aspect of Yolanda's selfhood demonstrates the way that everyone in her life seems to divide her into parts, often along the lines of her ethnicity and language. When their marriage falls apart, Yolanda writes to John that she needs "*some space, some time, until my head-slash-heart-slash-soul*—No, no no, she didn't want to divide herself anymore, three persons in one Yo" (78). The name Yo is the Spanish word for *I* in English, emphasizing Yolanda's dis-integration of self, a triple consciousness of both how the men whom she loves perceive her and how she perceives herself. In ¡*Yo!*, Dexter sees Yo as "American as apple pie. Well, let's say, as American as a Taco Bell taco" (194). Comparing her to a bland U.S. version of Mexican food, Dexter, as Rudy had done in college, conflates language with her national and cultural identity. For Dexter, as for Rudy, this conflation is gendered; Dexter believes Yo is "[s]ometimes the woman's libber, sometimes the Spanish inquisition" (192), stereotypes that deny her a personal motivation for her refusal to sleep with Rudy or her lack of interest in returning to Dexter. She must explain even to her third husband that "I'm not *Spanish*! I'm from the D.R. People in Spain would probably think of me as a . . . a savage" (*¡Yo!* 262). Yolanda's identity in exile is complicated by the Spanish colonial history of the Dominican Republic—the homeland of her homeland. The men in Yolanda's life ascribe everything she does to her ethnicity, which robs her of a personal identity. These identities— Yolanda's life and the one perceived by these men in the United States— deny Yolanda the integration of her own experiences and personality as a Dominican American woman living in the United States.

Asymptosy thus comes to represent Said's contention that exile is a "discontinuous state of being" (140). In the same way that the spaces of an exile's life remain separate and unassimilated, so does the exile's identity. In the same way that Yolanda cannot recuperate her Dominican identity when she visits the Dominican Republic because she meets her family's resistance to her independence, so is she unable to assert a fully "American" identity because of her Dominican past. The places of her life both contribute to and disrupt her identity, and she finds only dis-integration of the multiple contradictions of her life as a woman. Yolanda, writes Ellen Mayock, "is deeply troubled by her geographical past and present, by the cultural implications of that geography, by the constantly evolving mosaic of the combination of two distinctly different cultures" (223). For Yolanda, geographies are identities. Moreover, in the same way that Alvarez renders Minerva's displacement as internal and Camila's as both psychic and physical, so Yolanda's displacement and dis-integration stem from Alvarez's conception of asymptosy as a paradigm for interpreting and understanding identity in exile. ⌒

English as a Homeland

Language, Creativity, and Improvisation

Alvarez has found that exile—even with its contradictions—has allowed postcolonial women writers to achieve their identities as artists: "Our emigrations from our native countries and families helped us to achieve an important separation from a world in which it might not have been easy for us to strike out on our own, to escape the confining definitions of our gender roles" (*Something* 174). In her conception of the potential empowerment of exile, Alvarez reveals an important connection between exile and creativity.

As creative acts of language, her fiction, poetry, and essays reflect Alvarez's construction of language as a space in itself, a location in which to improvise identity in exile. In the essay that concludes her poetry collection *Homecoming*, Alvarez writes that she can see, in retrospect, the significant role language has played in her creative life. Even the young poet of the *Homecoming* poems, Alvarez writes, "surely knows where her roots really are—deep in the terra firma of language" (120). In the epigraph to the same book, she quotes Czeslaw Milosz's assertion that "Language is the only homeland." Alvarez later explains that "what Milosz meant was that the ability to create a place and feel like you belong in the human family happens through language." She had discovered at a young age, when her family was forced into exile, that she no longer wanted "to sink my soul in a piece of land, a national culture, because I had seen how quickly that could go." Instead, what she found was that "[l]anguage was a portable homeland" (Lyons and Oliver 135), and it was in "that portable homeland where I wanted to belong" (Alvarez, *Other Side* 117). Improvisation becomes an assertion of agency in postcolonial contests for space and nation. The space of this new homeland is a creative space of improvisation because, as Alvarez writes in *Something to Declare*, "in coming to this country and this new language, I discovered new resources and the need for self-invention" (145). This need for self-invention characterizes both the gendered dis-integration of exile and her experience with the English language.

The representation of the experience of exile exists within language itself. In *After Exile*, Amy Kaminsky sees language and space as a "mutual constitution," embodied in the production of language. "The prediscursive sense of rootedness," she suggests, "and the trauma of displacement, followed by learning new space, find their counterparts in the representation of fictional or poetic space, wherein language provides the means to establish as well as to recover a sense of place" (58). Elaine Savory makes clear the link between language and exile when she adapts Edward Said's "traveling theory"[1] to illustrate the exile's "'traveling identity,' a series of consecutive selves" ("Ex/Isle" 171). For women in the condition of what she calls "ex/isle," "language is itself a traveling space or series of spaces" (171). Language becomes for Alvarez something fluid and mutable, allowing and even sustaining the accumulating identities of women in exile. Exile is a series of liminal spaces, which Alvarez renders through narrative as a space of improvisation and possibility at the same time that it remains fraught with cultural and linguistic dissonance. Language is what connects Alvarez to that series of spaces that define her life—New York City, Vermont, the Dominican Republic.

Language has emerged as perhaps the most salient element of identity for writers defined by ethnicity, exile, or diaspora. Isabel Álvarez-Borland in "Displacements and Autobiography in Cuban-American Fiction" argues that in the adoption of the language of the exile's new country, the writer becomes a writer in diaspora—not in exile—a condition that weakens the writer's connection to the homeland. This discursive transformation is generally presented as a progression, a desired evolution in identity that presupposes acceptance, assimilation, and integration. In her work on Cristina García's *Dreaming in Cuban*, for example, Álvarez-Borland suggests that because García's childhood "occurred in English," she is able to "integrate issues of past and present more easily. As one of the first ethnic Cuban-American writers, García envisions questions of identity and heritage with less anxiety and thus greater distance from her material," giving her the ability to "walk the path from exile to ethnicity" (48). That path, as Álvarez-Borland portrays it, marks the culmination of an advantageous progression from exile writer to ethnic writer, suggesting a psychological wholeness unfettered by issues of multiculturalism—linguistic or otherwise. Kaminsky also envisions this progression from Spanish to English as psychologically and culturally salubrious, suggesting that "[i]n today's United States this embrace of ethnic identity does not mean a denial of origins, but rather a fuller participation in the cultural life of the new country" (134).

In the same way that hybridity may be fundamentally reductive as a paradigm for reading Alvarez's work, the putative progression from "exile to ethnic" may also obscure elements of the exile experience by highlighting assimilation and integration. In her excellent article on ethnicity and writing, "Contesting Boundaries of Exile in Latino/a Literature," Marta Caminero-Santangelo challenges "the construction of mutual exclusivity between exile and ethnic writing" (507). In Alvarez's work in particular, she finds that "critics who distinguish between 'exile' and 'U.S. ethnic literature'" have difficulty characterizing Alvarez's work—particularly *In the Time of the Butterflies*—because "the critics don't *expect* Alvarez to be writing an exile novel; as someone who came to the U.S. as a *child*, not an already developed writer, she 'should' be writing U.S. ethnic literature" (510). For Alvarez and other Latina/o writers, Caminero-Santangelo concludes that "exile and ethnic are permeable and overlapping categories" (513). Alvarez clearly considers herself a writer in exile—a theme and label that she uses repeatedly throughout her writing—as well as an ethnic writer who locates her comunidad among other U.S. Latina writers.[2]

Paramount in such discussions of ethnicity is language, the overlapping dimensions of ethnicity and exile that emerge in Alvarez's own experience of negotiating the spaces of English and Spanish. Alvarez remembers herself "[a]s an adolescent immigrant" who was "embarrassed by the ethnicity that rendered me colorful and an object of derision" (*Something* 165), largely because of language differences. As a result, Alvarez writes that she felt the loss of "the values and customs, the traditions and language that were an increasingly hidden part of me" (165). For Alvarez and her sisters, "the problem was that American culture, as we had experienced it until then, had left us out, and so we felt we had to give up being Dominicans to be Americans" (167). The negotiation of both of these cultures for Alvarez centers on language.

Writing about "My English," Alvarez points out that she has in fact come to see this second language as her own. Her mother "always used the possessive [adjective]: *your* English," as if the language were "an inheritance we had come into and must wisely use" (*Something* 24), as well as an individualized tool for self-creation. English had been an inheritance in a way; Alvarez's mother had learned English in American boarding schools and had passed the language on by sending her own girls to a small, American-run, English-language school in the Dominican Republic. Before attending that school, Alvarez had associated English in some way with the terror of the trujillato because her parents spoke in English when they did not want the children to understand their whispered worries and plans. "What I first recognized was not a language," Alvarez writes, "but a tone of voice; serious, urgent, something important and top secret." The result was that "[f]rom the beginning, English was the sound of worry and secrets, the sound of being left out" (22). Her experience with English in the United States would reiterate this lesson in exclusion, at least initially.

Perhaps as a result of her parents' use of English, Alvarez from an early age had an awareness of her own language—Spanish—as well. Because, as children, they "spent most of the day with the maids," Alvarez and her sisters "picked up their 'bad Spanish'" (21). The "bad Spanish" that the maids spoke was "a lilting, animated campuno," which Alvarez now claims as "my true mother tongue, not the Spanish of Calderón de la Barca or Cervantes or even Neruda, but of Chucha and Iluminada and

Gladys and Ursulina" (21–22). Alvarez here rejects standard Spanish, associated in her description not only with colonialism but also with a long tradition of male authors, men who defined, controlled, and enforced the standards of the language. Pedro Calderón de la Barca, a seventeenth-century Spanish playwright, and Miguel de Cervantes, the sixteenth-century Spanish author of *Don Quijote*, both represent for Alvarez the tradition of the *conquistadores* as well as the male-dominated canon of Spanish-language literature. In distancing herself from "even [Pablo] Neruda," a Nobel Prize winner and Chilean poet, Alvarez seeks to create a new space for herself and her "mother tongue" that is not governed by the language of colonial discourse and tradition. Alvarez instead embraces the language of the *campesinas*, the servants in the household, in an important demonstration of female solidarity that, in this case, appears to cross rigid class boundaries. She wants to write the female experience and so claims a "female" and anticolonial language to which she traces her early understanding of language; as a mother tongue, this *campuno* serves as the foundation for Alvarez's art in English as well. Alvarez thus engages in a process of decolonization, which must, as Savory asserts, "begin in language. It has to be directed towards regaining a creative cultural space after the confinements of colonization" ("En/Gendering Spaces" 12). The confinement that Alvarez recalls in both the Dominican Republic and the United States is mitigated by language.

Although Alvarez has claimed the power of this campuno as an adult and as a writer, class hierarchies in the Dominican Republic caused her some linguistic anxiety as a child. When she eventually began to attend the American school in the Dominican Republic, Alvarez "grew insecure about Spanish. My native tongue was not quite as good as English" (*Something* 24). At school, Spanish words seemed to her "illegal immigrants trying to cross a border into another language" (24). When they moved to the United States, the whole family spoke "mix-up," or "what's now called Spanglish" (24), for several years. In the Alvarez family, "[t]here wasn't a sentence that wasn't colonized by an English word" (24). These two images—border crossing and colonization—resound in

Alvarez's multiple experience with Spanish. It is indeed the language of the conquistadores who colonized the Caribbean, but, when she takes the language to the United States from the Dominican Republic, she is treated herself as if she is crossing a border into a country where she does not belong and where, in fact, she is not welcomed by its inhabitants. "When we immigrated to the United States in the early sixties," she writes, "the climate was not favorable for retaining our Spanish" (61). At the Catholic school she attended in the United States, "there were several incidents of name-calling and stone-throwing, which our teachers claimed would stop if my sisters and I joined with the other kids and quit congregating together at recess and jabbering away in Spanish" (62). With these admonitions, their teachers encouraged the rejection of both family and language in order to achieve assimilation.

As a result of the unfavorable climate for other languages, her early schooling in English, and the mysteries the language held in both her family and her school, Alvarez ultimately claimed the American English of the United States. In so doing, English "became a charged, fluid mass that carried me in its great fluent waves, rolling and moving onward, to deposit me on the shores of my new homeland" (*Something* 29). In adopting this new language as her own, "I was no longer a foreigner with no ground to stand on. I had landed in the English language" (29). At this point, language becomes for Alvarez a space of her own.

Claiming English as her new homeland had its cost: she began to speak her native Spanish with an accent. When the family would make return trips to the Island, Alvarez and her sisters increasingly spoke English, which she came to see as "a measure of the growing distance between ourselves and our native culture" (*Something* 64). In retrospect, Alvarez seeks to cast this distance from Spanish as empowering, "a way in which we were setting ourselves free from the old world where, as girls, we didn't have much say about what we could do with our lives" (63). For Alvarez, there is a gendered tension between exile and home, English and Spanish, and out of this tension she creates a narrative in which identities can be contested and redefined.

The linguistic space that Alvarez creates is primarily a narrative space. "What finally bridged the two worlds for me," she observes, "was writing" (*Something* 167). Looking for a way to be a Dominican and an American writer, Alvarez stumbled on Maxine Hong Kingston's *The Woman Warrior*, a book in which Hong Kingston "addressed the duality of her experience, the Babel of voices in her head, the confusions and pressures of being a Chinese American female," and Alvarez realized that writing multiple cultures "could be done!" (168). She later discovered the growing comunidad of Latina writers who were addressing similar issues of identity and displacement in their work. Through them, Alvarez observes "a whole group of us, a tradition forming, a dialogue going on," becoming for these Latinas "our own made-in-the-U.S.A. boom" (169). She sees herself as part of a full-fledged tradition, which she describes in an interview: "Nicholasa Mohr and Lorna Dee Cervantes were the first ones out there, clearing the ground. Then Sandra Cisneros, Ana Castillo, Denise Chávez, Cherríe Moraga, Helene María Viramontes, and the rest of us came. Now, new blood!" (Kevane and Heredia 30). Among these writers, Alvarez at last "found a comunidad in the word that I had never found in a neighborhood in this country" (*Something* 169–70). Alvarez's ties to this comunidad in the word rests primarily in language.

As a site of contestation over issues of identity and community, language is transformed by the exile into a transitional space. In this same way, Alvarez creates a narrative space through language that is itself transitional, focusing on the interstices between the speaker and the listener, the writer and the reader. Because this site is transitional, it is marked by improvisation. According to Benítez-Rojo, improvisation is closely tied to the Caribbean experience, particularly for the Caribbean writer. Improvisation, he writes, is "the easiest vehicle to take" to achieve the Caribbean poetic (21), reflected in the "aesthetic experience" of the Caribbean peoples, which "occurs within the framework of rituals and representations of a collective, ahistorical, and improvisatory nature" (22). Improvisation allows women in exile to deploy the identities imposed on them in new ways, innovating rather than integrating a multiplicity of identities. R. Keith Sawyer argues in "The Semiotics of Improvisation" that improvisation is both a contingent performance and a collective phenomenon (270). Conceived as both contingent and collective, improvisation allows the women in Alvarez's work to perform their Caribbean and American identities while they simultaneously retain community and identity. Moreover, improvisation allows Alvarez's women characters to assert their own agency, an agency that in turn enables them to resist the cultural erasure and implied role integration that the term "hybridity" suggests.

Improvisation has marked Alvarez's own experience in exile. Almost immediately she realized that "in America, you didn't go by what your family had been in the past, you created yourself anew" (*Something* 115). She develops this creativity throughout her novels, constructing the means through which women may respond to the dis-integration of exile. In Alvarez's novels of exile—*How the García Girls Lost Their Accents, ¡Yo!,* and *In the Name of Salomé*—Laura García de la Torre, her daughter Yolanda, and Camila Henríquez reinvent themselves repeatedly out of language and the constituent parts of their experiences at home and in exile.

Language and Exile

The tension in Alvarez's fiction between English and Spanish reflects the tension between the space of the island and the space of the United States. The title of her first novel, *How the García Girls Lost Their Accents,* focuses exclusively on language and plays on Alvarez's memories of her accent in both English and Spanish. For the García girls, language becomes a space for their new identity, a measure by which assimilation is measured, and a gendered feature of exile. Ibis Gómez-Vega points out that "in their new country, [the García girls] have neither a definable space nor an acceptable language with which to communicate" (87). Joan Hoffman sees "the struggle with language in the novel" as a means of "highlight[ing] the need to find the strength and self-assurance to forge an assimilated dual identity" (22). As both Gómez-Vega and Hoffman point out, the question of language cannot be separated from the spaces of nation and identity. Alvarez interrogates such questions of language, nation, and identity through improvisation, particularly in relation to Yolanda and her mother.

In the novel, language, according to Miryam Criado, is also a matter of absence: "La novela presenta, además, los problemas de incomunicación" (195). [The novel presents, moreover, the problems of noncommunication.] Criado also constructs a relationship between language and space by using a spatial metaphor to describe the circumstances of the García girls in exile when she argues that the García girls "desterraron de su lenguaje" [have uprooted from their language] (203). Criado's verb—*desterrar*—is related to *el destierro*, the dis-connection between self and ground, translated as exile. Distance in space from their (home)land becomes a distance from their language, culture, and identity as well. The apparent contradiction between *incomunicación*— not enough language or space—and traditional notions of multiculturalism and multilingualism—too many languages and too many spaces—is resolved through the improvisation of a new space, so that the multiplicity of experiences of *el destierro* can be interpreted and reconstructed to foster women's creativity.

The relationship between language and exile is clear in the first chapter of *How the García Girls Lost Their Accents* when Yolanda returns "home" to the Dominican Republic. Finally convincing her family to "allow" her to travel the island alone, Yolanda sets out across the country. Stopping in the small village of Altamira, Yolanda is suddenly taken by a craving for guavas, and she becomes stuck in a guava grove with a flat tire. As she waits for a local boy to return with help, two campesinos arrive with machetes. When they ask her what is wrong with the car, Yolanda feels that her tongue "has been stuffed in her mouth to keep her quiet" (20). Frightened, she admits to being American—not Dominican—and "the admission itself loosens her tongue," allowing her "to speak, English, a few words, of apology at first, then a great flood of explanation" (20). Alvarez says of this scene that Yolanda is "so un-at-home now that she can't even read the signals" (Lyons and Oliver 138). The distance between her and the campesinos is one of nationality, language, gender, and class, and because she no longer identifies herself as *dominicana*, she is unable to bridge that gap, to read, interpret, or send the appropriate signals. Only when she mentions the name of distant relatives who live locally do the campesinos begin to understand her and, finally, to repair her flat tire. Family—with its concomitant class status—is the only language they share in common. This incident is the first scene of the novel but chronologically the final scene of the García girls' story, and Alvarez begins with it in order to demonstrate the result of the journey that follows in the novel. The story is first and last one of language.

This first scene is echoed in events that occur earlier in time but later in the novel. In the adult Yolanda's marriage to John, who calls her "Joe," Alvarez focuses on Yolanda's many names to demonstrate her multiple identities. Yolanda is "nicknamed *Yo* in Spanish, misunderstood *Joe* in English, doubled and pronounced like the toy, *Yoyo*—or when forced to select from a rack of personalized key chains, *Joey*" (68). Yolanda is silenced by these nicknames, particularly by John's insistence on imposing and enforcing them. He calls her Violet—for shrinking violet because she sees a psychiatrist—and Josephine as well as Joe, until "her real name no longer sounded like her own" (79). The nicknames create further distance between Yo and her self, and this distance separates Yolanda fully from her language. The multiple names, and the confusion of identities that they represent, destroy Yolanda's marriage and lead her to be hospitalized.

In the hospital Yolanda looks back on the break-up of her marriage and understands the way language has helped her to construct and to lose a series of identities: woman, wife, writer. The first time John tells her that he loves her, Yolanda "was afraid. Once they got started on words, there was no telling what they could say" (72). She seems specifically to be afraid of English words. When John and Yo play rhyming games, in which he always creates and monitors the rules, she wants to be the sky, instead of the squirrel he has nicknamed her. He refuses, telling her sky does not rhyme with Joe. She replies, "*Yo* rhymes with *cielo* in Spanish," allowing her to run "like the mad, into the safety of her first tongue, where the proudly monolingual John could not catch her, even if he tried" (72). John represents many of the "proudly monolingual" citizens of the United States that immigrants and exiles face in their new lives; the Americans' refusal to speak another language reflects a deeper refusal even to accept another language as valid or meaningful. Language is not only a separate space for Yolanda, but it is also a safe space in which she can distance herself from John. As Yolanda imagines retreating into the safe space of Spanish, Alvarez evokes the double consciousness of Yolanda's cultural identity; Yolanda begins to see herself as Other through John's eyes. Using Spanish equates her with "the mad" because John draws a parallel between Yolanda's use of Spanish and insanity, snapping at her when she uses Spanish, "What you need is a goddam shrink!" (73). His anger in this scene reveals his fear that Yolanda may inhabit a space to which he has no access. Even in English, John does not believe in the power of words in the same way that Yolanda, the poet, believes. Instead, "he believed in the Real World, more than words, more than he believed in her" (73).

This opposition between words and the Real World manifests itself in their marriage through linguistic incompatibility. The first sign for Yo that she and John speak different languages comes when she discovers his list of pros and cons for marrying her. He tells her, "My way is to make lists. I could say the same thing to you about words" (74). He sees lists, however, as a rational and reasonable approach to problem solving, whereas he sees Yolanda's "words" as emotional and meaningless in the Real World. During their argument, he tries to kiss her, and Yolanda realizes that he is using that kiss to silence her. When "she opened her mouth to yell, No, no! [h]e pried his tongue between her lips, pushing her words back in her throat" (75). This silence—the anti-language he is trying to impose—allows John to control her and limit the spaces available to her as well. Ultimately, Yolanda no longer understands the language John speaks at all. After another argument, John comes home with flowers, but when "he handed them to her, she could not make out his words." She repeatedly asks him, "What are you trying to say?" She recognizes that "[h]e spoke kindly, but in a language she had never heard before" (77). Trying to imitate what she hears him saying, Yo "mimicked him. 'Babble babble babble babble'" (78). She desperately wants to "start over, in silence" (78), a place safer even than her native Spanish when she claims it for herself.

After leaving John, she goes to her parents' home, and her mother "diagnoses" Yolanda as "carried away with the sound of her voice" (79). At home, "[s]he talked too much, yakked all the time. She talked in her sleep, she talked when she ate" (79). Her parents then commit her to a psychiatric hospital. There, she continues to use language as an anti-silence, refusing John's power to silence her. At this point, however, Yolanda is not speaking her own language; she is mimicking the language of others, specifically male writers—the only tradition that she knows. Yolanda "quoted Frost; she misquoted Stevens; she paraphrased Rilke's description" (79). She "quoted *Don Quijote* in the original; she translated the passage on prisoners into instantaneous English" (80). The doctor tells her worried parents, "It's just a poem" (80). This dismissal of the art to which Yolanda has dedicated her life as a poet echoes John's dismissal of her words in favor of the Real World.

At the hospital, Yolanda imagines that her condition is improving, which she believes rests in the doctor's ability to "save her body-slash-mind-slash-soul by taking out all the slashes, making her own whole Yolanda" (80). When her parents come to visit, she quotes the doctor himself, telling her parents that crying is "a good sign," but quickly realizing that she is "quoting others again, a bad sign" (81). Yolanda decides to try her own words. "'I love you guys,' Yo improvised. So what if her first original words in months were the most hackneyed. They were her own truth" (81). Finally able to explain to her parents the reason for the break up of her marriage, Yo tells them, "We just didn't speak the same language" (81). Not speaking the same language becomes a pivotal moment for Yolanda as both a Caribbean woman in the United States and as a writer. Turning to improvisation, Yo uses language as a way of healing and reconciling her multiple identities. Although language may be used against her, in the way that John, her doctor, and even her parents wield nicknames against her and her sense of self, Yolanda realizes that she herself can use language to protect herself and, more important, to define herself. Finally, "[t]he words tumble out," and she realizes that "[t]here is no end to what can be said about the world" (85).

Yolanda's troubles with language in relationships had begun with Rudy Elmenhurst, the college boyfriend who had tried unsuccessfully to seduce her. Although Rudy sees the problem of their relationship as Yolanda's refusal to sleep with him, Yolanda explores the mystery of "why I didn't just sleep with someone as persistent as Rudy Elmenhurst" by "picking it apart the way we learned to do to each other's poems and stories in the English class" where they had met (*García Girls* 87–88). When their professor assigns the class to write a sonnet, they write it together. Yolanda is the one with the technical expertise, "writing down lines and crossing them off when they didn't scan or rhyme," while Rudy provides the ideas (93). For Yolanda, "[i]t was the first pornographic poem I'd ever co-written; of course I didn't know it was pornographic until Rudy explained to me all the word plays and double meanings" (93). Because English is still "a party favor for me—crack open the dictionary, find out if I'd just been insulted, praised, admonished, criticized" (87), she has difficulty decoding both the language of the poem and Rudy's intentions. He makes his intentions clear, but in a language that Yolanda rejects. Rudy talks about Yolanda's "getting felt up," prompting Yolanda to understand that "[h]is vocabulary turned me off even as I was beginning to acknowledge my body's pleasures" (96). The lesson Yolanda learns is not only about courtship but about her art. She comes to understand that although she had reserved poetry "for deep feelings and lofty sentiments" (93), poetry can be a space in which to record the experiences of her life.

The understanding that Yolanda comes to about language and poetry makes it clear that this novel about exile and the loss of accents is the story of Yolanda's coming into creativity. Yolanda's early experience with Rudy Elmenhurst demonstrates the connection she ultimately makes between writing and identity: Yolanda learns to mitigate the disintegration and the accumulation of her identities through writing. When her mother begins to sense Yolanda's dis-ease in New York, where "the natives were unfriendly," she decides that Yo "needed to settle somewhere" (141). For this reason and because nothing else makes sense to her, Yolanda "took root in the language" (141).

LANGUAGE AND IMPROVISATION

The improvisational nature of Yolanda's coming into creativity reappears in ¡Yo!, a novel that interrogates her writing from an outside perspective. In the novel, Yolanda García's family and friends are outraged that she has improvised fiction from their real experiences. Such an improvisation reflects Alvarez's own insistence on blurring the divisions between genres. To her sisters' criticism, Yolanda responds by asking, "What's art going to mirror if it isn't life?" (9), insisting on the link between her real experiences and her creative life. Fifi continues to believe that Yo is "talking about our family like everyone is some made-up character she can do with as she wants" (3), which betrays Fifi's own lack of control and emphasizes Yo's agency in the construction of her own life. Yolanda's lover, Doug, sees her "fabrications" as "not just about saving someone's feelings or her ass. It's as if the world is her plaything and she can just pick up the facts and make them what she wants" (195). Doug's loss of control over Yolanda's language is more frightening for him as a man than for Yolanda's sisters. The control that he is unable to wrest from Yolanda results in his beginning "to doubt everything she's told him" (195), which places the responsibility on Yolanda for lying and allows him to remain in control of what is factual—that is, the Real World, or the Truth.

Each of the characters in ¡Yo! seems to be aware that Yolanda is creating a life for herself through her writing, but their interpretations of the value of this self-creation differ somewhat. A more positive reading of Yolanda's writing comes, surprisingly, from her father, who ultimately comes to terms with his daughter's breaking of the silence mandated for women. He tells Yolanda, "Your destino has always been to tell stories. It is a blessing to be able to live out your destino" (295). He wants her to see, as he does, that "her books [are] her babies, and for me, they are my grandbabies" (294). In order to come to terms with Yolanda's breaking of silence and of tradition by getting divorced twice and rejecting motherhood, he casts her writing into the sanctioned paradigm of maternity, equating the creativity of mothers with Yolanda's creativity in her writing.

The connection between Yolanda's writing and her life is more disturbing for others in her life. Her cousin Lucinda tells her that Yo is "the haunted one who ended up living your life mostly on paper" (53). In high school, Lucinda is sent back to the Dominican Republic from her boarding school in the United States because of something Yolanda has written in her diary, which her mother reads and reports to Lucinda's family. Lucinda angrily tells Yo, "I hate how you snitched and made it look like you were just being creative. How you used your pen to get back at me. How your writing is one big fucking excuse for not living your life to the fullest" (231). Lucinda sees the creative world of the page as somehow inferior to a life lived "to the fullest" in what she, like both John and Doug, perceives as the Real World. Doug himself sees Yolanda's creativity as a way to control her life, in which the "momentary inspirations" she picks up "she eventually deletes from the rough draft of her life" (272–73). The notion that Yolanda has the ability to revise her life as a work in progress emerges as paramount for Alvarez's narrative space. Alvarez's own work reveals the improvisatory process of writing, as in the final sonnet of "33" in the reissue of *Homecoming*:

> Sometimes the words are so close I am
> more who I am when I'm down on paper
> than anywhere else as if my life were
> practicing for the real me. (102)

"Practicing for the real me" is an exercise in improvisation, located in the narrative space of her work.

As with Alvarez, Yolanda's writing is the means by which she creates new identities as a Dominican woman living in the United States. Even as a child, storytelling had defined her. Yo has always believed, her mother says, that "the truth is just something you make up" (¡*Yo!* 12), and she has always had "that need to invent" (34). Yolanda's improvisation is rooted in language, as a woman who "is never at a loss for words" (194). As a young girl, Yo also "had to have the last word" (31), an early desire for voice and, consequently, power in a culture that did not allow it for girls. Echoing the Garcías' maid Chucha in *How the García Girls Lost Their Accents*, Hoffman suggests that even in exile "Yolanda still has spirit in her; she still has her art, her writing, her refuge. With that she will always be able to invent what she needs to survive" (26). The ability to invent comes from Yolanda's mother, a gift that Alvarez reveals as a parallel to her own life. In the preface to the reissue of *Homecoming*, Alvarez explains that "[i]n writing *Homecoming*, I can see now how fiercely I was claiming my woman's voice. As I followed my mother cleaning house, washing and ironing clothes, rolling dough, I was using the material of my housebound girl life to claim my woman's legacy" (119). The "material" of Alvarez's life emerges in the improvisatory space of her writing, which she represents in Yolanda's inheritance of the mother tongue and the ability to invent what she needs to survive. Such an improvisation allows Alvarez to redefine housework to include and value all the work that women do in the home: cooking, cleaning, loving, organizing, storytelling, inventing, and writing.

Her mother's appreciation for Yolanda's "need to invent" comes from her own efforts at improvisation as well. Laura García's improvisation is, like Yolanda's, firmly rooted in language. Although Laura's English is better than her husband's, she struggles with the language's idioms.[3] Taking various pieces of English slogans, slang, and clichés, Laura improvises new phrases, creating new meanings for trite sayings and platitudes in English. She speaks "a mishmash of mixed-up idioms and sayings that showed she was 'green behind the ears.'" When her husband insists that "she speak Spanish so the girls wouldn't forget their native tongue, she'd snap, 'When in Rome, do unto the Romans'" (*García Girls* 135). Such resistance to her husband "was like sheets hitting a fan" (23), making it "hell on the wheels of our marriage" (26). While her husband struggles to become in the United States the doctor that he had been in the Dominican Republic, Laura notes that Papi "was studying like cats and dogs for his license exam. We were living on the low end of the hog" (29), stuck in an apartment that makes them feel like "more sardines in a can than you could shake a stick at" (49). Her revision of these clichés represents her efforts to improvise her life out of two conflicting parts of her experience in exile—English and Spanish. While she makes herself understood, her language also identifies her as an outsider, despite her attempts to assimilate. Moreover, as a primary marker of national identity, language and her difficulties with it become an obstacle to assimilation, demonstrating linguistically her dis-integration in American culture.

Perhaps because "*[n]ecessity is the daughter of invention*" (142), Laura turns to inventing—literally. On weekends she visits department stores, where "[d]own in housewares were the true treasures women were after" (*García Girls* 133). She browses the aisles, improving on the devices she sees there, improvising by combining and reinventing uses for them. Studying the sketch of one of her mother's improvisations, Yo guesses: "Soap sprayed from the nozzle head of a shower when you turned the knob a certain way? Instant coffee with creamer already mixed in? Time-released water capsules for your potted plants when you were away? A keychain with a timer that would go off when your parking meter was about to expire?" (137). The significance of Laura's inventions lies in the combination of other ordinary devices in the same way that the most ordinary of language—clichés and proverbs and platitudes—provides the tools for her to assert her own language to describe and experience her new life in exile.

Despite Laura's desire to invent, she puts her role as mother first, and "[s]he never put anything actual on paper until she had settled down her house at night" (134). The girls, however, see their mother differently:

"None of her daughters was very encouraging. They resented her spending time on those dumb inventions. Here they were trying to fit in America among Americans; they needed help figuring out who they were" (138). On the other hand, "'Better she reinvents the wheel than be on our cases all the time' the oldest, Carla observed. In the close quarters of an American nuclear family, their mother's prodigious energy was becoming a real drain on their self-determination" (139). Conflicted about the dis-integration of Laura's identity as Mami and as a mom, the girls oscillate between being resentful and grateful for their mother's attention to her inventions. Her daughters mock her as "something of a family joke, their Thomas Edison Mami, their Benjamin Franklin Mom" (137). With only white, American, male role models like Thomas Edison and Benjamin Franklin, the girls cannot imagine their mother as an inventor, a role that does not fit their Dominican image of Mami. They are unable to appreciate, or even to understand, their mother's improvisation in regard to their own self-construction in the United States. Although they are in the process of remaking themselves, Laura's daughters resist revising their image of motherhood, perhaps demonstrating that improvisation is essentially an elaboration of the self rather than a categorical transformation of experience.

The elaboration of self that Laura attempts eventually conforms to more traditional notions of Dominican womanhood, ultimately leading Laura to stop inventing. Yo and her father fight over a speech that Yo has written to honor the teachers at her school. She quotes Walt Whitman, invoking freedom of thought and speech, but her father explodes, reflecting an inheritance of the trujillato—silence, conformity, and exaggerated demonstrations of respect. When he tears up Yo's hard work, she is forced to rewrite the speech quickly, and Laura turns the energy that she had used for inventions to rewrite Yo's speech. This "speech her mother wrote [was] her last invention. It was as if, after that, her mother had passed on to Yoyo her pencil and pad and said, 'Okay, Cuquita, here's the buck. You give it a shot'" (149). Laura thus passes on the mother tongue to her daughter, a legacy of language that challenges the legacy of silence demanded by the father and the colonial, patriarchal world from which he comes. Ultimately, instead of inventing, "several days a week, dressed professionally in a white smock with a little name tag pinned on the lapel, a shopping bag full of cleaning materials and rags," Laura cleans and organizes her husband's office, and "at night she did the books" (140–41), gendered tasks that alleviate the conflict between Dominican expectations and her barely developed American identity as a woman. Laura's adherence to Dominican-defined gender roles may spring from her own desire to alleviate the stress that dis-integration causes her in exile.

When Laura gives Yolanda "the buck," she passes on more than just an interest in language. She provides Yolanda with the ability to conceive of herself as an agent in the construction of her world, passing on invention and improvisation for Yolanda's own desire to create and write. Even Yolanda's early storytelling can be traced back to her mother's storytelling, which characterizes the girls' memories of her. Mami "had a favorite story she liked to tell about each one as a way of celebrating that daughter on special occasions" (*García Girls* 42), and "[a]lthough she was not particularly religious, she liked to make her plots providential" (44). For Carla, Mami tells a story about Carla's desperate desire for a pair of tennis shoes. About Yolanda, she describes her talents as a poet. Her story about Fifi demonstrates how the family considers Fifi to be the lucky one. For the third sister, "[t]he mother does not tell a favorite story about Sandra anymore. [Sandi] says she would like to forget the past" (50). The stories represent for the girls the past, a Dominican past that they feel they must eventually forget—and reject—in order to live in the United States. These distinctions in time reflect the distance in space that Sandi and her sisters imagine lies between them, their homeland, and their prior identities.

The relationship between storytelling and time is not lost on Laura. She realizes in *¡Yo!*,

> Isn't a story a charm? All you have to say is, *And then we came to the United States*, and with that *and then*, you skip over four

more years of disappearing friends, sleepless nights, house arrest, narrow escape, *and then*, you've got two adults and four wired-up kids in a small, dark apartment near Columbia University. (28)

For Laura, a story is a way to revise her own life and leave behind her memories, the horrors of the trujillato, in the Dominican Republic, the location of the García past. That space of memory is eclipsed through storytelling as the Garcías invent a new life outside of the trujillato in both space and time. The revision of stories underpins Laura's belief that "[t]here's more to the story. There always is to a true story" (*García Girls* 102). Ultimately, even her father learns from Yolanda's creativity and invention in the same way that Yolanda had learned from her mother, discovering that "I can add my own invention—that much I have learned from Yo. A new ending can be made out of what I now know" (308). Alvarez's repeated use of the phrase "out of" in her renderings of Yolanda's and her parents' inventions and creativity demonstrates improvisation to be the paramount experience in their new place on the map, the English language.

In Alvarez's *In the Name of Salomé*, Camila Henríquez is also improvising a life in exile, disconnected from the Dominican Republic, from the memory of her mother, and from her own identity. In the novel, each of the stories of Camila's life takes place in a new location and in a new decade. Often she would decide "to try out a new life by writing to Marion about it" (189). These improvisations allow Camila to reinvent herself repeatedly during her life in exile: scholar, lesbian, poet, heterosexual, diplomat, teacher, revolutionary. In all her wandering, Camila realizes, "[i]t is my mother I am looking for" (242). The search for her mother's history becomes a search for her own history, both lost to her since childhood as the result of exile and death.

Because Camila's task is to go through her mother's papers for the national archive, Camila engages in a process of editing that allows her to improvise her mother's life and to invent one for herself. Although she feels herself "the nobody among them," Camila "will be the one editing the story of her famous family" (38). This ability to improvise her mother's life and, more important, her mother's memory in the collective history of the Dominican Republic, empowers Camila, a feeling that leads her to consider fleetingly, "let the true story be told!" by allowing everything to go to Salomé's archive (44). Believing that "[t]here are other women she can be besides the heroine of the story" (126), Camila innovates a series of identities in order to discover who that woman is that she can be. Collecting and editing the papers, notes, poems, and bits of her mother's life, Camila discovers "the details of Salomé's story that increasingly connect her mother's life to her own" (45). In improvising her mother's story out of fragments of memory, Camila also improvises her own life. In repeated discussions with another artist, Camila begins to understand the complex improvisation that memory and legend create: "[b]ack and forth they go, conversing and weaving the imagined fabric of Salomé's life from what Camila already knows and what she is discovering by talking openly with him about her mother" (160). Weaving proves to be an improvisational strategy for Camila, who weaves their lives together to effect the accumulation of their collective stories, the improvisation of exile.

Through sorting her mother's papers and reading her mother's poetry, Camila is "filling in the gaps left behind by her mother" (79). Camila consults "those poems for signs" (2), engaging in what her doctor calls "magical thinking" (31), perhaps a gentle term for Camila's special brand of literary criticism. And although Camila is, "after all, the anonymous one, the one who has done nothing remarkable," she finds that at poetry readings "she is in demand for sentimental reasons, the daughter who lost her mother, the orphan marched out in her starched party dress to recite her mother's poem[s]" (69–70). Significantly, Camila "is not above improvising on her mother's poems" (77). Camila's improvisation is an assertion of her own independence and identity as she adapts Salomé's words and ideas to fit Camila's needs at that moment in time. Improvising her mother's poetry allows her to step out from behind her mother's legend, even for just a moment, to shed light on who she wants to be. In the same way, Alvarez calls her own translations of Salomé's poetry "approximations/improvisations in English" (357), situating Alvarez's own work within this Caribbean tradition.

Memory plays an important role in Camila's improvisation of both Salomé's story and her own. For Camila, "[t]he truth is: she remembers spots. And the rest is the story she has made up to connect those few dim memories so that she does not lose her mother completely" (119). Unlike Laura García, who uses her improvised stories to dis-remember her life under Trujillo, Camila uses improvisation to create memories she does not actually have. Relying on the collective memory of the Dominican people, who knew her mother and her work but from whom Camila is disconnected through exile, Camila creates a narrative of her own life as well as that of her mother.

Improvisation draws on the tradition of colonial mapping from the seventeenth and eighteenth centuries, in which mapmakers had seldom visited or seen the islands that they constructed to represent the reality of those places; they improvised those maps, drawing from stories, histories, pictures, sketches, and accounts, and pulling them together into the space of the map. The sources of those maps, however, generally emerged out of a singular tradition: white, upper-class, Catholic men. Alvarez's new place on the map includes those people, experiences, and artistic traditions long absent from historical mappings of the United States, the Caribbean, and, in particular, the Dominican Republic. Moreover, the mappings that Alvarez inscribes stem from her own experiences and perspective, providing her with a modicum of autonomy insofar as she is mapping—not mapped. These improvisations of memory provide the foundation for Alvarez's interrogation of language as part of her narrative space. Alvarez complicates the character of her narrative space through this connection of memory and improvisation and reveals silence as much as language to characterize traditional notions about Dominican history and memory. ✐

SILENCE ON THE ISLAND

Recovering Collective Memory

On the island of Hispaniola, between Haiti and the Dominican Republic, runs the Massacre River, named for the slaughter of thirty buccaneers by Spanish colonials in 1728. The river earned its name again in 1937, when Trujillo ordered the massacre of thousands of Haitians living on the border in the Dominican Republic.[1] That river—and the countries it divides—provides a site for Alvarez's exploration of the relationship between place and collective memory where she can reveal the politics of collective memory on both sides of the Massacre River. "What happened at the Massacre River in 1937 is still vivid in the minds of the islanders," Michele Wucker writes in *Why the Cocks Fight*. "Even now, it is nearly impossible for Dominicans and Haitians to think of each other without some trace of the tragedy of their mutual history" (44). The politics of memory shape narratives of race, class, nation, and gender, mapping a national story that purports to represent all citizens. For Dominicans, particularly, remembering the regime that initiated such violence on both sides of the Massacre River—the trujillato—is a painful negotiation of race, nation, and identity. As Neil Larsen asks, "¿Como narrar el trujillato?"—how do we narrate the Era of Trujillo?—we also ask, how do Dominicans remember, and commemorate, the trujillato?

Alvarez reveals in her historical novels—*In the Time of the Butterflies*, *In the Name of Salomé*, and *Before We Were Free*—that collective memory is multiple. Alvarez suggests that, like postcolonial constructions of identity, collective memory is an accumulation of personal and family memories, history, commemorative practices, and individual and cultural experiences.

Trujillo himself understood the power of collective memory and shaped it for his particular use in both the present and his imagined future. He commemorated himself frequently and on a grand scale: monuments, parades, and rituals were devoted entirely to him, earning him, for a time, a place in the *Guinness Book of World Records* as the leader who built the most statues in his own honor (Wucker 69). Those commemorations were the space Trujillo claimed in which to construct the national identity of the Dominican Republic, his attempt to shape the country's collective memory and identity. He required his portrait hung in every household, with an accompanying text: "In this house, Trujillo is chief." "The most humiliating of these [public assertions of power]," Alvarez writes, particularly for Dominican men, were "the occasional parade in which women were made to march and turn their heads and acknowledge the great man as they passed the review stand" (*Something* 106). Such demonstrations allowed Trujillo to exert control over both the men and the women—all of whom were someone's wife, daughter, mother, or sister—without risking confrontation with Dominican men. He often used these parades to inspect the women, any of whom he might choose as a mistress. These ceremonies were mandatory if Dominicans wished to have stamped their *cédulas*, identity papers that allowed them whatever small movement they might be allowed throughout and beyond the country.

Theorists of collective memory have revealed two opposing constructions of both its function and location. Pierre Nora has argued that collective memory is attached to sites, which he calls *lieux de mémoire*, in contrast to history, which is attached to events (22). *Lieux de mémoire* are "simple and ambiguous, natural and artificial, at once immediately available in concrete sensual experience and susceptible to the most abstract elaboration. Indeed they are lieux in three senses of the word—material, symbolic, and functional" (18–19). These lieux are the very monuments that Trujillo constructed, the portraits he commissioned, and the ceremonies he commanded. Michael Shudson mitigates Nora's assertion somewhat by stressing that these monuments and markers "are *dedicated* memory forms, cultural artifacts explicitly and self-consciously designed to preserve memories and ordinarily intended to have general pedagogical influence" (347). In contrast to such sites, Susan Crane argues that collective memory is ultimately located in the individuals who do the work of remembering ("Writing" 1381). At issue here, in a sense, is the geography of collective memory.

In addition to the discussion of the location of collective memory, Alvarez anticipates another contemporary debate about the rigid distinction between history and memory. She takes part through her novels in discussions in historical scholarship about the distinction between history and memory. Kerwin Lee Klein points out that while it has very nearly become a cliché in memory studies to argue that history and memory are not oppositional constructs (128), the two often remain opposed in scholarly writings on the topic. In "(Not) Writing History," Crane refuses to create an opposition between memory and history, suggesting that "[h]istory is a form for collective memory" (21). Moreover, she blurs the distinctions between the "personal" and the "historical," which often "seem to be antithetical categories implying a distinction between private and public, opinion and fact, individual and collective" (6). These distinctions line up along gender boundaries, in which women are generally associated with the private, the collective, and opinion, particularly in societies in which the individual is highly valued. Such distinctions, feminist scholars have long argued, create gender and social stratifications that directly affect women's access to power. In traditional constructions of history and memory, women are associated with memory, which is often confined to the domain of female culture. James Fentress and Chris Wickham have found that in "most Western societies, women, rather than men, have the responsibility of encapsulating (sanitizing, moralizing) accounts of the experienced past for young children, as part of the process of socialization" (142). The influence of Western societies in the colonial history of the Caribbean has created a variety of island cultures in which women are charged with the perpetuation of the "experienced past"—memory—as is apparent in the work of such Caribbean writers as Edwidge Danticat,

Jamaica Kincaid, and Cristina Garcia as well as Alvarez.[2] The experienced past corresponds to the personal—the family and the community—rather than the national, creating the same binary division that Crane seeks to dismantle. Alvarez herself writes that in Dominican culture "[i]t was a woman's place to be the guardian of the home and the family secrets, to keep things entre familia" (*Something* 122). Gendered in this way, the collective memory that Alvarez writes reveals national identity and history through women's eyes, in stark contrast to masculinist versions of history and traditional historical memory, which focus on the lives, actions, decisions, deaths, and wars of men. The distinction between history and memory thus creates divisions of gender, race, and nationality, ultimately devaluing collective memory as inferior to the "objective" events and materials of history. "By creating a new pattern of looking back at historical events," writes Gus Puleo, "which is, retrospectively, the creation of a new memory—the Dominican writer corrects the past" (13).

In his paean to the lives and deaths of the Mirabal sisters—*las mariposas*—at the hands of Trujillo, Pedro Mir makes a significant connection between memory and monuments, which represent or, some argue, actually contain the collective memory of the sisters for the Dominican people.

Es que
hay columnas de marmol impetuoso no rendidas al tiempo
y piramides absolutas erigidas sobre las civilizaciones
que no pueden resistir la muerte de ciertas mariposas.
[It's that
there are columns of impetuous marble that are not worn down
    by time
and solid pyramids erected in the name of civilizations
that cannot withstand the death of certain butterflies.]

He calls for a remembrance of the Mirabales that rivals the permanence of marble columns and great pyramids. Such a site would not only provide a focus for the collective memory of a country, but it would also appear on the country's maps, particularly maps for tourists, who are often outsiders. As part of her project to write a new place on the map, Alvarez, like Mir, explores the collective memory located in the monuments, markers, and museums of the Dominican Republic, while simultaneously including those missing from previous maps of the country's history.

History is, of course, a mapping of the past, both of which have long traditions across a variety of cultures and centuries. As John Lewes Gaddis writes in *The Landscape of History*, "The making of maps must be as ancient and ubiquitous a practice as is our three-part conception of time. Both reduce the infinitely complex to a finite, manageable, frame of reference. As with the writing of history, maps also "distill the experiences of others" (32) in the "packaging of vicarious experience" (33). The connection Gaddis makes here exposes the underlying project of writing history and making maps as it pertains to Alvarez's work: reducing culture to a "manageable" entity that can be defined and controlled by the few people who have historically had access to publication and thus the construction and dissemination of knowledge. Alvarez seeks not to distill the Caribbean experience but to expand it.

In her own historical writings, Alvarez relies on both les lieux as constructed by Nora and the individuals in the novel as the force behind the construction of the memory of the trujillato. The sites of memory and individual stories about the Mirabal sisters and the Ureña women combine to create the crowded narrative arena of their history. This cacophony informs the multiplicity of Alvarez's collective memory and rejects both silence and the master narrative of a single History. Alvarez's new place on the map seeks to reveal the discontinuities of singular versions of both history and memory and to write the multiplicity of both the Dominican past and present. Distinctions between them are subordinated to her greater project of writing both history and memory into her fiction. Yet she refuses to blend these concepts or the stories that emerge from them—as theories of hybridity would dictate—into a unified whole or a single voice. The voices of the Mirabal sisters, Salomé Ureña, and Camila Henríquez destabilize monologic discourses of Dominican history. A construction of collective memory that accounts for a multiplicity of locations and manifestations mitigates the need for rigid distinctions between sites and individuals, and between individuals and community. Alvarez's vision of collective memory textualizes history and memory, the vernacular and the official, fiction and fact. Such a vision also reveals a collective memory that expresses a national identity that includes all members of the memory community. Alvarez, in remembering both the trujillato and the tumultuous years that preceded it in Dominican history, reconceives collective memory as existing in a shared space (the narrative) and in the individual (the narrators).

Silence on the Island

In remembering and restoring lost or absent collective memory, Alvarez responds to the mandated political silence that has long characterized island culture, notably in regard to women's experiences and contributions. As Ruth Behar points out in a review of *In the Time of the Butterflies*, "The history textbooks tell the story of Spanish America's bloody struggles for independence, decolonization, and freedom as if women were never there, as if women had no place in the nation and in history" (6). The absence of women in historical narratives parallels gaps in official collective memory of the nation. Like Alvarez's work, recent campaigns of remembrance in the Dominican Republic also seek to redress this forgetting. Alan Cambeira points to Dr. José Francisco Peña Gómez, leader of the *Partido Revolucionario Dominicano*, as a driving force behind "the case for remembrance" (178). Cambeira translates Peña Gómez's mandate that "[i]n order to be an authentic and complete Dominican, it is necessary to preserve a lasting and unalterable memory of the vicissitudes and deterioration suffered on the part of the national personality, in every sense, during the Era of Trujillo" (178). Dominicans today "are being reminded constantly that the Trujillo Era, which saw the country turn into a tightly run prison camp, operated under the absolute control of a single man" (179). That single man also mandated a single history.

Much of Alvarez's writing plays a part in the "case for remembrance," creating a collective memory out of the blank spaces of forgetting that Trujillo and other dictators attempted to impose. In *Something to Declare*, Alvarez presents her own family's experiences under the trujillato. In the essay "A Genetics of Justice," in particular, she provides personal memories and historical information about the years of the dictatorship and the Alvarez family's subsequent exile. She notes, however, that

> my parents rarely spoke about the circumstances of our leaving the Island. To us, their daughters, they offered the official story: my father wanted to study heart surgery. We were not told that every night our house had been surrounded by black Volkswagens; that the SIM had been on the verge of arresting my father; that we had, in fact, escaped to the United States. (108)

The need for an "official story" stems from the way that "my parents, along with a nation of Dominicans had learned the habit of repression, censorship, terror" (107). This habit followed them into exile in the United States, where "[e]ven on American soil, they were afraid of awful consequences if they spoke out or disagreed with authorities" (108). The imposed silence of dictatorship has its counterpart in the misuse of language. "Misusing the language," Alvarez writes, "is something that dictatorship and totalitarian governments know all about. One of the first things such a regime does is to seize control of the media, to censor the stories of the people, to silence dissenting opinions. I grew up when there was only one story—the official story" ("Ten" 39). Alvarez's use of language to break the silence of dictatorship is a response to that official story. While Trujillo used language to manipulate and control Dominicans, he demanded their silence, except for those willing to inform on their neighbors.

Alvarez sustains the relationship between silence and control throughout *In the Time of the Butterflies*. Under the trujillato, Alvarez writes, Dominicans dreaded "words repeated, distorted, words recreated by those who might bear them a grudge, words stitched to words until they are the winding sheet the family will be buried in when their bodies are found dumped in a ditch, their tongues cut off for speaking too much" (10). As Minerva's friend Sinita points out, "people who opened their mouths didn't live very long" (18). The Mirabal family thus recognizes the power of silence in the trujillato. In their efforts to protect Minerva, who interests Trujillo at first personally and later politically, her family repeatedly silences her, providing her with their own words, which they see as less dangerous for her. Mate writes a speech for Minerva praising El Jefe at the Salcedo Hall, which "worked, too. Suddenly, she got her permission to go to law school" (121). When Minerva is called to SIM headquarters in the capital city, her mother, who generally "doesn't say a word in public" (106), speaks for her, saying, "All my daughter wants is to be a good, loyal citizen of the regime" (114). Later, at a command performance for Trujillo, a lavish party that the Mirabales are "requested" to attend, "Papa says to Minerva, 'you keep quiet'" (93), and Patria begs her, "*Ay, Minerva, por Dios*, keep that tongue in check tonight" (94). After Minerva is imprisoned and released, she must seek permission to visit a doctor. Patria, aware that the SIM is always listening, speaks for her, saying, "'And you would be very grateful for the captain's leniency in allowing you to go' Patria reminded me, embedding my request in her scold" (272). Finally, in one of the most poignant scenes in the novel, as Minerva and Dedé are traveling together, they are pulled over by five *calíes*. Minerva says, "I will never forget the terror on Dedé's face. How she reached for my hand. How, when we were asked to identify ourselves, what she said was—I will never forget this—She said, 'My name is Minerva Mirabal'" (277). Dedé speaks for Minerva, willing to take her sister's identity and risk the punishment meant for Minerva.

Language becomes a tool for Trujillo's political control. The underground June 14th Movement, which Trujillo tries to quash, is compromised by language and silence, leaving Minerva to lament in prison that the "movement is falling apart with all this mistrust and gossip" (244). After Minerva and Mate are released, Trujillo, knowing the effect his words will have on the growing resistance movement, announces to a large group of people at a party, "My only two problems are the damn church and the Mirabal sisters" (281). Reporting Trujillo's words to the girls, as is Trujillo's intention, their uncle tells them, "If he was really going to do something, he wouldn't have announced it. That's the whole point. He was giving me a warning to deliver back to you" (281). Whether Trujillo's intention changed or not, the warning is both a caution and an omen; the Mirabal sisters will be killed. Even after the sisters are murdered, Alvarez insists on the role of language as she describes the way the sisters' husbands learn about their "accident": "Johnny Abbes and Cándido Torres and other top SIM cronies were waiting, already quite drunk. This was going to be a special treat, by invitation only, a torture session of an unusual nature, giving the men the news" (332). Language is here not only a political tool but also a weapon of torture.

Growing up in such an environment, Alvarez remembers that their family also lived by her mother's proverb: "'En boca cerrada no entran moscas.' No flies fly into a closed mouth. Later, I found out that this very saying had been scratched on the lintel of the entrance to the SIM's torture center at La Cuarenta" (*Something* 109). By alluding to the political prisoners tortured by Trujillo and his henchmen, Alvarez evokes the large-scale resistance to his regime that flourished all over the island— a resistance signified in the act of silence. This double reading of the inscription at La Cuarenta demonstrates the dictator's tool deployed against him. Such reversals lie at the heart of resistance. Alvarez links her own family's experience to that tradition of resistance and survival. In writing her books, Alvarez participates in the resistance in her own fashion, breaking the mandate of silence imposed by dictatorship. "[I]f I shut up," Alvarez asks, "wouldn't I still be fanning the embers of the dictatorship with its continuing power of censorship and control over the imagination of many Dominicans?" (111).

Alvarez's family stories also reveal the connection between personal and national memories, blurring restrictive distinctions between individual and community experience. In "Silver Linings," she recalls the connections her mother has made between family and history. According to Alvarez's mother, "I was born under a bad star. All the major events of my life had an uncanny way of coinciding with natural, national, and international disasters." Alvarez broke her right arm "the very morning Trujillo was assassinated," her mother tells her (77). In the family photograph album, "[u]nder each snapshot of me in my first communion dress or blowing out ten candles or holding up my spelling bee trophy, a caption is written out in my mother's hand: 'June 5, 1967: Julia's graduation. Arab-Israeli 6-day war starts.'" Her mother also points to "a snapshot of me looking very demonic in a black gown and unraveling a scroll in front of an ivied wall. 'Julia earns Masters diploma,' the caption reads. 'May 16, 1978, coup in Santo Domingo'" (78). These photographs comprise the material history that often evokes and informs memory; the connection between nation and family demonstrates the accumulation of history and memory that Alvarez seeks as she maps the Dominican Republic for her North American audience. Throughout her personal writings and her novels, Alvarez suggests that family history cannot be extricated from (inter)national history. Her personal essays, *In the Time of the Butterflies*, and *In the Name of Salomé* are all family stories; by privileging family over nation, literature over history, and memory over material and archival evidence, Alvarez inverts traditional hierarchies of value.

Remembering the Dominican Republic

Of all of her novels, Alvarez's *In the Name of Salomé* explores the most distant past—the nineteenth century and the independence of the Dominican nation. Beginning with the birth in 1850 of la poetisa nacional, Salomé Ureña, and ending with Camila Henríquez's return to Santo Domingo in 1973, the novel probes the silence not only of the Era of Trujillo but also of the unstable governments and dictators who preceded him. Salomé lives by the same code as the Alvarez family, writing of the political situation at home to her husband in France, "I had better say no more. As we know, no flies can enter a closed mouth" (214). The lesson that Salomé has learned about silence comes from the horrors she has witnessed during the years that the Dominican Republic struggled to be una patria. During a government sweep for weapons in 1881, for example, Salomé's "Tía Ana opened the top of the Dutch door and told them we had all the weapons we needed: Salomé's poems and Christ, our Lord." To this apparent dissidence, the police responded by shooting in the street a neighbor who had a revolver hidden in his boot. After that, "Tía Ana seldom said a word. I believe she felt responsible for a martyrdom she might have prevented" (182). Such acts of violence create a culture of silence, one instantiated in the Dominican Republic long before Trujillo ascended to the presidency.

The silence of *In the Name of Salomé* is gendered as well. As Salomé's reputation as a poet grows, she receives increasing attention from visitors, important dignitaries in the political and cultural life of the country—the archbishop, other writers, and even the president. During these visits, Salomé writes, "if I had something to say and there was enough silence for me to say it, I would speak up" (89). As the only woman among a group of well-known men, Salomé seldom has conversational space to break the silence imposed on her. "And so the rumor spread," she writes, "that Salomé Ureña was a woman who hardly talks" (89). Paradoxically, such silence might actually work in her favor; the fact that she repeatedly breaks the compulsory silence for women by writing poetry—specifically political poetry—would be mitigated by her social silence in the presence of these men.

Alvarez intends *In the Name of Salomé* as a way to break the silence imposed on Salomé, who is virtually unknown outside the Dominican Republic, and the silence concerning women as forces in Dominican history. In her acknowledgments, Alvarez writes that the book "is an effort to understand the great silence from which these two women emerged and into which they have disappeared." Writing the novel "enabled me to recover the history and poetry and presences of the past" (357), a multiplicity that characterizes her reconstruction of the Dominican and American memory of la poetisa nacional of the Dominican Republic.

In the novel, Alvarez writes her country's history through the perspectives of Salomé Ureña and Camila Henríquez.

Alvarez seeks to reclaim Salomé Ureña from the oblivion that has characterized Ureña's work in the academy and popular culture of the United States. In the novel, Camila's friend Marion tells her, "I honestly don't think I would have ever heard of your mother unless I had met you." For Camila's part, "[s]he's not surprised. Americans don't interest themselves in the heroes and heroines of minor countries until someone makes a movie about them" (7). Camila must also teach her Spanish students, who do not know Salomé, that she is "[a]s good as your Emily Dickinson, as good as your Walt Whitman." As she tells them about her mother, Camila "cannot forget the indifference in their voices, the casualness of their dismissal. Everything of ours—from our lives to our literature—has always been so disposable," (39). Alvarez is writing that "disposable" memory into permanence, commemorating for North Americans the work and life of Salomé Ureña and her daughter. On the other hand, for those Dominicans who are already familiar with Salomé and her work, Alvarez seeks to retrieve the woman from the myth, to reveal the asymptotic gap between constructions of her identity as la poetisa nacional and her identity as daughter, sister, wife, and mother.

Alvarez's novel for young adults, *Before We Were Free*, treats much of the same subject matter as Alvarez's other writings about the Dominican Republic, including the story of silence under Trujillo's regime. Twelve-year-old Anita de la Torre experiences both Trujillo's rule and his assassination, which Dominicans call the *ajusticiamiento*—a bringing to justice. Beginning in 1960, near the end of the trujillato and just before the assassination of the Mirabal sisters, everyone is always telling Anita to "shhhh!" Her Mami is always quoting one of the maid's sayings, "'No flies fly into a closed mouth.' The less said, the better" (26). This dictum, under which Alvarez herself grew up, forms a thread throughout the whole of her writings that suggests the ways she is working out the relationship between her writings and that silence. Under Trujillo, the maid Chucha tells Anita, there is "[n]o protection but silence" (50). At the American school that Anita attends on the island, their Secret Santa activities are cancelled because "some parents feel that there's enough tension in the air. Kids sneaking around and leaving secret messages might be taken the wrong way." Anita's Mami tells her, "There are enough secrets" on the island already (33).

Anita, like Salomé and Camila, breaks the silence that threatens to engulf her when she records the events of her life and her country in her diary, blurring the lines between personal and national history and emphasizing the multiplicity of Dominican collective memory. Initially, her efforts to escape that silence are tentative. "I always write with a pencil for a reason," she records. "I want to be sure that on a moment's notice I can erase what I've written." She lives with the reality that "[w]ith a few strokes back and forth, I can get rid of any evidence if the SIM come to the door." In such a climate, both writing and living are difficult for Anita, who feels "kind of sad writing in pencil, always prepared to erase" (43). When she feels "like my whole world is coming undone," she can turn to her diary and "my pencil is a needle and thread, and I'm stitching the scraps back together" (48). Alvarez herself uses her novels for adults and for children to stitch together the scraps of memory that have survived the terror of the trujillato.

Eventually, Anita must stop writing in her diary, a figurative silencing of voice that extends to her literal voice as well, as she begins speaking less and less frequently. Her linguistic memory begins to disappear—as her Tío Tony has disappeared, as her cousins have disappeared to the United States—and she finds "I can't come up with the words" (86). Feeling unsafe and voiceless, Anita feels "the words slide away from my memory" (88). She comes to see herself as "the girl who hardly talks anymore" (92), feeling as if "the words are stuffed inside my mouth like a gag keeping me from talking" (99). Her silence, however, may empower her after all, as she recognizes that it may, paradoxically, be her way of "voicing a silent protest" (82). When she is allowed to write in her diary again, Anita's memory returns: "The words are coming back, as if by writing them down, I'm fishing them out of forgetfulness, one by one"

(111). For Anita, writing is a way of preserving memory, of recording "the story of what is happening to us" (124). Language becomes the way for history to become recorded, to be written into existence. When Anita's father is killed in the bloody aftermath of Trujillo's assassination, her mother tells the Counsel General, "'Tell!' Mami orders. 'I want to hear how they died. I want my children to hear this. I want my country to hear this. I want the United States to hear this'" (151). Such is the function of *Before We Were Free*, and Alvarez's other novels of the Dominican Republic as well. She writes into the memory community both Dominicans and Americans, breaking the silence of the country's history and breaking down national and geographical boundaries that perpetuate oppression and silence.

The lessons of the trujillato also appear in Alvarez's novels of exile, which depend on memory for the reconstruction of those lessons. In *How the García Girls Lost Their Accents*, Alvarez writes that the García girls had learned "the national language of a police state: every word, every gesture, a possible mine field, watch what you say, look where you go" (211). This "national language" is learned through a series of lessons in the Dominican Republic, continuing into their exile in the United States. The scene in which Yolanda inherits the ability to invent, improvise, and create from her mother reveals another lesson for the García girls about life in a police state. When Yolanda writes that speech to honor her teachers, her father objects to the entirety of the speech, shouting, "What is wrong? I will tell you what is wrong. It shows no gratitude. It is boastful. *I celebrate myself? The best student learns to destroy the teachers?*" He finds the speech "is insubordinate. It is improper. It is disrespecting of her teachers" (145), and he forbids her to deliver it. Ultimately, "he tore the speech into shreds" (146), an action that prompts his wife to tell him, "This is America, Papi, America! You are not in a savage country anymore" (146). Laura recognizes immediately that his anger is masking what he truly feels—fear. Yolanda, however, is distraught. She does not realize that "her father had lost brothers and friends to the dictator Trujillo." She does not yet recognize that

[f]or the rest of his life, he would be haunted by blood in the streets and late night disappearances. Even after all these years, he cringed if a black Volkswagen passed him on the street. He feared anyone in uniform: the meter maid giving out parking tickets, a museum guard approaching to tell him not to get too close to his favorite Goya. (146–47)

In her misapprehension of her father's anger, she "thought of the worst thing she could say to her father. She gathered a handful of scraps, stood up, and hurled them in his face. In a low, ugly whisper, she pronounced Trujillo's hated nickname: 'Chapita! You're just another Chapita!'" (147).[3] What the displaced and disillusioned Yolanda does understand is that her father's behavior is somehow connected to their lives in the Dominican Republic, but without thinking of his haunted past and what he has lost, she equates his actions with those of the man responsible for Carlos's fear. Later, he tells her, "I just want to protect you" (149). In his desire to protect his daughter, he initiates his own mandate of silence, even for their new lives in the United States.

Because the events in *How the García Girls Lost Their Accents* appear in reverse chronological order, the early events of the trujillato that Yolanda remembers occur later in the book. In "The Blood of the Conquistadores," the first chapter in the final section of the book, the action takes place just before the Garcías' flight from the Dominican Republic. In this chapter, Alvarez describes what eventually leads to Papi's mandate of silence for his own family, events that Alvarez invented in order to provide herself with a missing memory. In an interview, Alvarez has said that the "story 'Blood of the Conquistadores' was one that I really had to write because I have no memories of our last day on the island. I think it's the pivotal event in my life, and I can't remember a thing that happened" (Wiley 9). Memory, Alvarez says, is "tricky" because "memory is already the story you made up about the past" (10). Alvarez clearly believes what Andreas Huyssen suggests in *Twilight Memories*: "The past is not simply there in memory, but it must be articulated to become memory" (2–3). Alvarez articulates the event in fiction in order to claim a memory she does not possess.

In "Blood of the Conquistadores," Alvarez reiterates the culture of silence that pervaded the island under Trujillo. The girls' "Mami says they're not to tell their friends" about their father's involvement with the man they call "Tío Vic," who turns out to be an agent with the CIA. "'No flies fly into a closed mouth,' she explains when Carla asks, 'Why can't we tell?'" (309). Memory plays an important role in this silence as well; Yolanda has learned the lesson of silence not from her mother's proverb but from remembering "the time Yoyo told their neighbor, the old general, a made-up story about Papi having a gun, a story which turned out to be true because Papi really did have a hidden gun for some reason." Possession of an illegal gun could have meant imprisonment or death for Carlos García, and to teach Yolanda—to make her remember—"her parents hit her very hard in the bathroom, with the shower on so no one could hear her screams" (198). Her parents insist on the silence necessary in the trujillato, simulating it themselves with the shower when Yolanda cannot remain quiet during her lessons in silence. To make sure she understands the lesson, her father beats her with a belt. Carlos recalls, "All I could think was that I had to silence our betrayer." Her silence would be guaranteed by the beating and the accompanying litany, "You must never tell stories" (*¡Yo!* 307). Yoyo apparently learns the lesson well because when Trujillo's military police arrive for the final time, provoking the Garcías' exile, "Yoyo does not say a word" (*García Girls* 198).

Alvarez expands this incident through Carlos Garcías's voice in *¡Yo!* He is loath to remember the incident, to tell the story, "a story I have kept secret because it is also a story of my shame" (296). He feels he must tell the story, however, so that he can, for the family and the Dominican people, rescind the injunction of silence by which their lives had been governed so that Yolanda may take pride in her *destino* as writer and storyteller. But he is also reluctant because of "one of those lingering habits of dictatorship when we censored all of our stories" (307). At the time of Yolanda's punishment, "[w]e were living in terror, and I reacted with terror. I beat her. I told her that she must never tell stories again" (296). Significantly, Carlos imagines that his memory of the event is not certain; time has interfered as well as Yolanda's writings. "I have read the story of those years over and over as Yo has written it, and I know I've substituted her fiction for my facts here and there" (299). In this "second" story, Carlos provides details absent in *How the García Girls Lost Their Accents*.

In *¡Yo!*, Carlos remembers, "The undoctored truth is that I joined the underground." He also "kept an illegal gun" (299). These two facts had put not only him at risk but his family as well. When Yolanda reveals the gun's existence to General Molina, the García household is frantic. Seeing her parents so upset causes Yo to realize "that a story could kill as well as cure someone" (305). After the beating, after a sleepless night, and after realizing that the general has not reported them to Trujillo and the SIM, Carlos goes to Yolanda's room, where she has cried herself to sleep. He says, "I tried but I could not speak. It was as if the injunction of silence I had laid on her had also fallen on me." For Carlos, "[i]n my memory of that moment, there are no words" (308). Many years later, after Yolanda has published a fictional first novel loosely based on her own experiences, Carlos wants to ensure that she feels that there are words for her to tell her story.

Alvarez reveals most deeply her concern for collective memory and the legacy of silence in the Dominican Republic in her novel *In the Time of the Butterflies*. Set entirely in the Dominican Republic, this novel focuses exclusively on the trujillato. The novel recreates the lives of the real Mirabal sisters—Minerva, Patria, and María Teresa—and their assassination in 1960. Alvarez writes their lives through their own voices and through the voice of Dedé, the surviving sister, who is "the grande dame of the beautiful, terrible past" (*Butterflies* 65). Although Behar sees her as "the history-weary Dedé" (7), Jacqueline Stefanko has suggested that Dedé's survival in the novel "lies in the negotiation of personal and collective history because by surviving, Dedé enables memory, the narration of the stories of Las Mariposas. Remembering is explicitly characterized as narration as Dedé constructs her sisters" (62). Elizabeth Coonrod Martínez calls this "a collective historicization," which is enabled by "[r]ecalling the past, and bringing common people into national perspective with a novel" (271–72). Alvarez explicitly conceives the novels as collective: Dedé remembers "our tragedy—because it is *our* tragedy, really, the whole country's" (*Butterflies* 312), and this collectivization of Dominican memory and history allows "[t]hese women characters [to] claim the memory and the authority for the telling of their story" (Martínez 272).

The paradox of the Mirabal sisters' story is that Alvarez has to retrieve it not from the silence of the trujillato but from the profusion of post-Trujillo narratives about las mariposas. Alvarez must clear or create a space in which to gather these myths and legends and to add one of her own. Resisting the claims to a single national narrative that Trujillo had made with his own monuments and rituals, the Dominican people have answered that tradition with their own narratives about las mariposas, contained in the monuments and markers that have proliferated since their assassination. The interaction between narration and collective memory produces a story that commemorates the Mirabales, not Trujillo himself. In the author's note at the end of the novel, Alvarez states that she has sought to write "not the Mirabal sisters of fact, or even the Mirabal sisters of legend" (324). In her search for the butterflies, she realized that "deification was dangerous, the same god-making impulse that had created our tyrant. And ironically, by making them myth, we lost the Mirabals once more, dismissing the challenge of their courage as impossible for us, ordinary men and women." Finally, she hopes to have captured "the true spirit of the Mirabals" (324).

The word "legend" suggests a story, a narrative invented for instruction or entertainment. Both history and legend, however, represent the past and work to bind together a community who share that past. Legends can limit our understanding of the Mirabal sisters in Dominican history because they fail to provide a complex narrative of their lives and risk reinforcing and recreating a single, monolithic fiction. Drawing on legend, history, and memory, Alvarez seeks to release the Mirabal sisters from the confines of legacy. Alvarez points to narrative as a way of reconciling both history and legend, memory and myth, in the story of las mariposas, and creating the multiplicity of collective memory that contests traditional constructions of the Mirabal sisters' lives. Such a conception of narrative as a means of understanding history allows for the inclusion of the multiple discourses of myth, memory, and history.

Alvarez is also engaged in the process of retrieving the Mirabal sisters from masculine discourse. A representative of the values of this discourse, Roberto González Eschevarría berates Alvarez's departures from "actual history" in his review of the novel for the *New York Times Book Review*. He writes:

> The actual history in 'In the Time of the Butterflies' is very blurry. I find no connection between the specific dates Ms. Alvarez gives to mark periods in the Mirabals' lives and either Dominican or broader Latin American history. Serious historical fiction establishes links between individual destiny and pivotal political events. (18)

His suggestion that her novel is not serious historical fiction also seems to hinge on what he perceives to be "too much crying in the novel" (18). Calling it "maudlin," he writes that Alvarez "clutters her novel with far too many misdeeds and misfortunes: rape, harassment, miscarriage, separation, abuse, breast cancer" (18). The (gendered) "clutter," coupled with the book's lack of "specific dates" from "actual history," reveals the androcentric bias of Eschevarría's construction of "serious historical fiction." His review only accentuates Alvarez's efforts to write the Mirabal sisters as women and not merely the Mirabal sisters of legend. As Concepción Bados Ciria has noted, the Mirabal sisters "appear in Alvarez's novel not as the sisters of a legend, wrapped in superlatives and ascended into myth, as they still continue to appear in works written by men" (412); instead, Alvarez engages in what Alicia Ostriker has called revisionist mythmaking, common among women poets. Ostriker sees "the core of revisionist mythmaking" as lying in "the challenge to and correction of gender stereotypes embodied in myth" (318). Alvarez addresses such stereotypes in her portrayal of the sisters as women when she demonstrates that stereotypes can create a sort of asymptotic relationship to the self. Alvarez explores the ways that Minerva struggles with her multiple identities as daughter, mother, wife, revolutionary, leader, and hero, a dimension of the Mirabal myth not often the center of narratives of their lives.

Dedé's belief that the tragedy belongs to the whole country echoes Alvarez's own sense of being haunted by the sisters' lives and deaths. In December of 1960, just four months after her own flight from the Dominican Republic, Alvarez discovered a *Time* magazine article about the sisters' assassination. "And so it was," she writes, "that my family's emigration to the United States started at the very time their lives ended." The acts of these three women and their husbands "stood in stark contrast to the self-saving actions of my own family and other Dominican exiles" (*Something* 198). She began to connect her own escape with their deaths. Such a connection increases the risk of silence; as Ellen Fine has argued in her work on post-Holocaust writing, "For those born in the shadow of genocide, apprehensions about their right to speak are often linked to the guilt of nonparticipation" (43). Writers in these conditions "are haunted by the world that has vanished; a large gap exists in their history, and they desire to bridge this gap" (43). Echoing Fine's analysis, Alvarez writes, "The Mirabal sisters haunted me. Indeed, they haunted the whole country" (*Something* 198). Perhaps out of the guilt that Fine identifies, Alvarez found that the story of the Mirabales "seemed almost impossible for me to write. It was too perfect, too tragic, too awful. The girls' story didn't need a story" (202). But she "wanted to understand the living, breathing women who had faced all the difficult challenges and choices of those terrible years. I believed that only making them real, alive, could I make them mean anything to the rest of us" (203). Only through writing could Alvarez bridge the gap in her own and her country's history.

Only through fiction could Alvarez conceive the sisters' memory.

Part of the story of the Mirabal sisters is the story of the time in which they lived, which is dominated by the single figure of Trujillo. The pervasiveness of Trujillo's construction of his own image is apparent in the many biographies published about him during his lifetime. A 1957 biography of El Jefe, *Trujillo: A Biography of a Great Leader*, published under the auspices of the Dominican government and written by Abelardo R. Nanita, "Senator of the Republic, Former Secretary of the President, Former Member of the Cabinet, etc.," unsurprisingly presents a picture of "the upright and heroic figure of Generalissimo Trujillo" (viii). In contrast to more recent histories of Trujillo's reign, Nanita asserts that "the country's peace has known no disturbance since Trujillo took power" (103). In *The Land Columbus Loved Best*, a vast history of the country published for a North American audience, Bertita Harding also praises the safety and peace that Trujillo brought to the country, the streets of which "are safer at night than those of a small American town, and crime has sharply decreased" (56). Neither Nanita nor Harding seems to comprehend that peace and enforced silence are not the same thing. Harding ultimately concludes without irony that "General Trujillo has permanently marked the pages of history" (51). Readers of these two books, however, gained no knowledge of the deepest, most devastating marks left by Trujillo in Dominican history.

Alvarez brings these pages of history into her novels in order to offer alternative versions. In *In the Time of the Butterflies*, Minerva Mirabal learns in her classes in 1944 the official story about Trujillo from her "new history textbooks with a picture of you-know-who embossed on the cover," books that begin with these words: "The 24th of October in 1891, God's glory made flesh in a miracle. Rafael Leonidas Trujillo has been born" (24). From her classmate Sinita, most of whose family had disappeared or died as a result of speaking out against the regime, Minerva comes to understand an alternative history—that "Trujillo was doing bad things" (17). Minerva's new understanding of the trujillato is accompanied by the onset of womanhood; soon after Sinita shares the truth, Minerva realizes, "Sure enough, my complications had started" (20). The transmission of knowledge about Trujillo is thus gendered in Alvarez's rendition. Alvarez not only couples knowledge with menstruation but she also transforms communities of women into agents of communication. The youngest Mirabal sister, María Teresa, had felt "so lucky that we have [Trujillo] for a president" (37), but as she comes toward womanhood, Minerva passes on to Mate what Sinita had shared with her. As with womanhood, Mate feels "so strange now I know something I'm not supposed to know. Everything looks a little different" (39). Knowledge about Trujillo is both collective and gendered, a way of knowing and understanding the world that suggests both physical and psychological changes.

The conflation of Trujillo and God is a motif that Alvarez uses in the novel to emphasize Trujillo's power in the Dominican Republic. When Minerva learns about Trujillo from Sinita, she feels "as if I had just heard Jesus had slapped a baby or Our Blessed Mother had not conceived Him the immaculate conception way" (17). That Minerva's new knowledge is linked so closely with her Catholic beliefs[4] points to the merging of Trujillo and God with Minerva's own values and religious beliefs. Alvarez returns to this idea later in the novel when Patria, the most devout of the sisters, builds an altar and prays to Trujillo for the release of her husband and son. Under "the required portrait of El Jefe," Patria sets "a vase on the table," joined soon by "a nice little lace cloth." At this improvised altar, Patria finds, "pretty soon, I was praying to him, not because he was worthy or anything like that. I wanted something from him" (202): the release of her family. Her mother believes that Patria "was just putting on a show for Peña and his SIM who came by often to check on the family," but she really "wanted to turn him towards his better nature" (203). Patria suffers the imprisonment of her family in silent prayer, unable to articulate aloud her desires to Peña, to Trujillo, or even to God.

COMMEMORATION, MATERIAL HISTORY, AND TESTIMONIO

Alvarez's novels of the Dominican Republic function as commemorative texts. Traditionally, commemoration is manifest in museums, parades, monuments, and other sites and ceremonies that provide a specific space in which to mark the memory of historical events and people. In practice, commemoration is frequently accomplished by designating an object, location, or ritual as meaningful, and those multiple meanings are both constructed and contested, as people assimilate them into the (hi)story they tell themselves about their nation. *In the Name of Salomé* incorporates one such commemoration, a weeklong festival at Salomé's birthday, at which Camila is invited to speak. In honor of her mother, "[t]he festival will conclude with a memorial service at her tomb, and Max has written that el Jefe will attend and unveil a fifty-cent coin with 'Mother's pretty portrait on it'" (71). These masculine traditions of commemoration, which Alvarez explores in *In the Time of the Butterflies* as well, focus on the grave—often a monument in the name of the Church—and the coin, which is actually an expression of the state. Alvarez revises these commemorative practices in her novel, focusing on narrative as a means of recovering and recreating collective memory. In the novel, Camila also chooses language to perform commemoration, breaking the silence mandated by Trujillo. At a speech about her mother's poetry, Camila says, "'I cannot celebrate my mother's work when her country is in shambles.' She brings up the murders, the massacre of the Haitians she has never mentioned publicly before. All her life she has had to think first of her words' effect on the important roles her father and uncles and cousins were playing in the world" (85). However, she continues, "if I remain quiet, then I lose my mother completely, for the only way I really know her is through the things she stood for" (85). Only in breaking the silence can Camila—and Alvarez—reclaim Salomé's memory and the collective memory of the regimes that sought to possess her and her memory for their own purposes. In the same way that Salomé becomes one of her husband's "grand and noble ideas" as Pancho recreates—prettying and whitening—her image, Trujillo with his festival and coin seeks to claim Salomé for the Dominican Republic as he defines it.

The commemorative space consecrated to the trujillato in Dominican history, however, is a masculine space, leaving little room for the iteration of women's memories. Martínez suggests that *In the Time of the Butterflies* itself "*remembers* forgotten martyrs" (270). Puleo notes that the novel "memorializes the brutal assassination of the Mirabal sisters" (11). Such insistence on retrieving and rewriting the memory of the Mirabal sisters has particular relevance for Alvarez's North American audience. At the time of their assassination, the few stories that appeared in U.S. English-language media outlets were strangely focused on Minerva's desirability. The *Time* magazine article to which Alvarez refers was published in the issue for December 12, 1960. The piece is accompanied by a photograph of Minerva with the caption "A slap on the seigneur's face." The caption refers to the article's statement that Minerva "reportedly caught the Dictator's eye some years ago when she was a pretty university student. When Trujillo tried to exercise his Dominican version of *droit du seigneur*, Minerva's response was a stinging slap on the face. Shortly thereafter, both Minerva and her middle-aged father were jailed" ("Warning" 32). A similar account appeared in *The New York Times* on November 30, 1960. The short article contained this allusion to Minerva's sexual appeal: "Two Dominican resistance organizations in New York reported yesterday that the Mirabal family's troubles with the dictator started about twelve years ago when Minerva Mirabal rejected his attentions" ("Wives" 5). The emphasis on this event focuses on Minerva's desirability and minimizes the pivotal role she played in the resistance movement; this approach suggests that she is a woman, not a rebel. Alvarez's novel demonstrates that Minerva's intelligence, wit, and connections were the "problems" facing Trujillo rather than his desire for revenge for sexual rejection. Alvarez's narrative not only corrects history, as Puleo has suggested, but it adds to the accumulation of narratives about Minerva's life. She writes into Minerva's story the details of a life that had heretofore been distilled into a single, widely reported slap.

Out of Trujillo's long tradition of commemoration emerge monuments and a museum dedicated to the Mirabal sisters and their resistance to Trujillo's dictatorship, monuments that themselves are social constructions of memory. National identity and memory are often located in museums, which are themselves, argues Irit Rogoff, "a twentieth-century critical discourse, a theorization of the cultural practices of collecting, classifying, displaying, entertaining, and legitimating various histories through selected objects within staged environments" (231). The critical discourse of the museum is a matter of national heritage, creating an official history of the nation. Even small museums, such as the one dedicated to the Mirabal sisters, shape the collective memory, in this case, of both the mariposas and of the trujillato in general. What is at stake, Crane argues, "in the current politically charged arena of museums and memory is distortion: distortion of 'the past,' distortion of the museum experience, memory distortions, and the negative charge associated with 'distortion' in cultural discourse on memory and identity" ("Memory" 57). Part of our cultural interest in museums as institutions of memory lies in our feeling of obligation "to collect remains, testimonies, documents, images, speeches, any signs of what has been" (Nora 13). These material artifacts of history can replace memory rather than represent it, rejecting the stories and experiences of those who do not have access to institutions of history. Mainstream museums, as locations and inventories of history, may also exclude the histories of the silent and invisible. If museums are to be what Crane calls "memory institutions," their discourses must legitimize testimony and experience—creating what Crane calls "the multiple pasts" ("Writing" 1382)—as much as documents and artifacts.

Museums generally reflect the narratives the nation tells itself about its origins, history, values, victories, and destiny. The museum, as Huyssen argues, has served "as catalyst for the articulation of tradition and nation, heritage and canon, and has provided the master maps for the construction of cultural legitimacy in both a national and universalist sense" (13). The connection Huyssen makes between the map and the museum demonstrates the extent to which both serve as discourses of a nation, which can be deployed against or in the name of that nation by those in power. The traditional museum "produces and affirms the symbolic order," one that in the Dominican Republic has been negotiated and renegotiated in the politically, economically, and socially tumultuous years since Trujillo's death. Moreover, Huyssen adds, "there is always a surplus of meaning that exceeds set ideological boundaries, opening spaces for reflection and counter-hegemonic memory" (15). Because the Mirabal museum opened after Trujillo's own assassination, it tells a different narrative than other sites created under his auspices.

The museum commemorating the Mirabal sisters is located in their house, a domestic space that immediately genders the country's collective memory of their lives. Alvarez writes in *Something to Declare*, "As I entered the Mirabal house, as I was shown the little patio where Trujillo's secret police gathered at night to spy on the girls, as I held the books Minerva treasured (Plutarch, Gandhi, Rousseau), I felt my scalp tingle" (199). Alvarez notes the "little clothes that the girls had made in prison for their children," their jewelry, their dresses, and Maria Teresa's braid (200). These artifacts of memory—jewelry, clothing, and hair—are also gendered markers of the sisters' identity as women rather than national heroines. Because "gender is a covert signifying process," Rogoff argues, the feminization of museums and their contents alters both memory and history. Rogoff has remarked that German museum displays of the Nazi era are sometimes feminized, "characterized by a disproportionately high representation of the lives of women, domestic economies, and the culture of survival" (231). This feminization of fascism emphasizes "the realities of women's lives (*civilian* lives), and focus[es] on the remains as *debris* rather than *ruins* and on the protagonists as *victims* rather than *vanquished*," thus rewriting "the entire relation of the nation to its fascist heritage" (italics in original 242). The feminization of the space of Dominican collective memory about the trujillato—the Mirabal museum and its contents—marginalizes the sisters in Dominican history, a decentering that Alvarez resists by providing them literary space in the novel that focuses on their whole lives, particularly their education and political activities outside the domestic space of the home.

Alvarez also relies on documents and sites—Nora's lieux—in her reconstruction of the memory of the Mirabal sisters. She has read the letters passed between Minerva and Manolo, documents of their relationship and experiences, and she "combed for information about the Trujillo regime" in the National Archives (*Something* 204). She and her husband visited the González farm, Minerva and Manolo's house in Monte Cristi, the family church, Minerva's friend Sinita's home, and the site of the "accident." "Everywhere we went," Alvarez writes, "it seemed we could reach out and touch history" (207). These sites allow Alvarez to touch history in a literal sense—the paper of letters, the stone of a church, the grass of a farm. In contrast to the silences imposed by the regime, Alvarez must carve out from the overcrowded space the Mirabal story.

The physical vestiges of history have traditionally lent legitimacy to individual memories of events, which might not otherwise be included as part of history. Alvarez recognizes the relationship between material remains and memory in *In the Time of the Butterflies*. Dedé, as the surviving sister, becomes the guardian of the girls' memory. She sets up the museum as well, "just five minutes away and everyone shows up there wanting to hear the story firsthand" (311–12). When the "gringa dominicana" arrives at the beginning of the novel, Dedé knows that the material memories—"books and articles [...] the letters and diaries" (7)—represent the expectations of those in search of history and memory; they are the stuff of the *gringa*'s "research." Before Dedé "knows it, she is setting up her life as if it were an exhibit labeled neatly for those who can read: THE SISTER WHO SURVIVED" (5). In the museum, there are also "three pictures of the girls, old favorites that are now emblazoned on the posters every November, making these once intimate snapshots seem too famous to be the sisters she knew" (5). For Dedé, those pictures are now markers of something else, not her sisters but the national heroines, icons of the trujillato.

The material history of the museum sparks other commemorative practices that purport to honor the sisters but merely serve to commodify them. Dedé dreads the time when, "[e]very year as the 25th rolls around, the television crews drive up. There's the obligatory interview. Then, the big celebrations over at the museum, the delegations from as far as Peru and Paraguay, an ordeal really" (3).[5] These ordeals—the commodifications of the sisters' assassination for public consumption in the media—are commemorative practices detached from the Mirabals as people, from the epoch they did not survive, and from the terror of the dictator who had them killed.

Other surviving remains of the sisters' lives come from the site of the accident, the belongings found in the car. Dedé takes an inventory of "[t]he losses. I can count them up like the list the coroner gave us" (314). She can

> say them like a catechism:
> One pink powder puff.
> One pair of red high-heeled shoes.
> The two-inch heel from a cream-colored shoe. [. . .]
> One screwdriver.
> One brown leather purse.
> One patent leather purse with straps missing.
> One pair of yellow nylon underwear.
> One pocket mirror.
> Four lottery tickets. [. . .]
> One receipt from El Gallo.
> One missal held together with a rubber band.
> One man's wallet, 56 *centavos* in the pocket.
> Seven rings, three plain gold bands, one gold with a small
>   diamond stone, one gold with an opal and four
>   pearls, one man's ring with garnet and eagle insignia,
>   one silver initial ring.
> One scapular of Our Lady of Sorrows.
> One Saint Christopher's medal. (314–15)

That Alvarez includes these gendered artifacts in the novel reveals her own consciousness of the domestic reality of these women's lives, in spite of what they represent to those in search of history. Alvarez is not feminizing their story to de-center it, but rather gendering the collective memory of the sisters to demonstrate the possibilities of history silenced by a single version of the events of Trujillo's regime. Moreover, these personal objects—unlike a sepulcher or a stamp—resonate with the details of their lives rather than their deaths.

Alvarez also reclaims these artifacts so that they are not marking the Mirabal deaths as much as they are celebrating their lives; such acts are demonstrations that Trujillo's power is being progressively reclaimed by the Dominican people. Trujillo's *Obelisco del Malecón*, for example, was constructed to commemorate the Trujillo-Hull Treaty of 1940.[6] On March 8, 1997, this obelisk became a monument to the Mirabal sisters when Dominicans painted a mural titled "Un Canto a la Libertad" commemorating the sisters over the obelisk itself, inscribing a new history atop the official one. Indeed, soon after Trujillo's assassination on May 30, 1961, "at the very spot on the renamed 30th of May Highway where the dictator died, they erected a memorial of concrete and twisted, rusted steel—a tribute to the pain he had inflicted" (Wucker 69). The tradition of monuments such as these, combined with the museum of the Mirabal home in Salcedo as well as libraries, statues, and parks dedicated to *las hermanas*, creates of the sisters a myth or legend. The mythologizing of the Mirabal sisters leaves us with many narratives and many memories, which Alvarez must take into account even while she is providing an additional construction of history, memory, and literature.

Among these narratives, Alvarez draws on the Latin American tradition of *testimonio*. As she explains in an interview,

> Certainly I was influenced by the literature of the Holocaust and the testimonial tradition that comes out of Latin America—the whole tradition, the Mothers of the Plaza in Argentina. I did a lot of reading of women in the Resistance during World War II. A lot of the reading I did is not part of North American literature, except for the narratives of slavery. Political testimonial literature does not come from the U.S.A.

tradition. It just goes to show that as a writer I am a mixture of traditions. (Kevane and Heredia 28)

Alvarez explicitly places *Before We Were Free* in this tradition, claiming that it is "the responsibility of those who survive the struggle for freedom to give testimony. To tell their story in order to keep alive the memory of those who died" (*Before* 166). *Testimonio* also plays a significant role in *In the Time of the Butterflies*. As Ellen McCracken argues, the novel "might be viewed as a kind of collective autobiography or testimonio of the women" (84). Alvarez also includes in the novel the testimonio of witnesses to the sisters' assassination. Just after the "accident," Dedé listens to the testimonies of those who had seen the girls on their last day. She says, "They would come with their stories of that afternoon," all wanting "to give me something of the girls' last moments." She creates memory from these witnesses' stories, "composing in my head how that last afternoon went" (301). Testimony becomes her memory.

Years later, Dedé is no longer the listener but the teller, testifying and witnessing to the girls' lives. She wonders when her life changed "from my being the one who listened to the stories people brought to being the one whom people came to for the story of the Mirabal sisters" (312). When Trujillo was assassinated and the country was plagued by a succession of unstable governments, Dedé tells a friend, "We were a broken people. [. . .] [I]nstead of listening, I started talking. We had lost hope, and we needed a story to understand what had happened to us" (313). In telling her own story and the story of her sisters and of the Dominican people, Dedé can pass on the memory to the gringa dominicana, who in turn passes it on to the English-speaking world in the novel.[7] In passing on the memory, by making it part of the collective memory, Dedé feels that "the future is now beginning. By the time it is over, it will be the past, and she doesn't want to be the only one left to tell their story" (10). In this way, testimony serves as part of the collective memory and as part of the healing process of those who survived Trujillo's regime.

As Michael Bernard-Donals and Richard Glejzer tell us in *Between Witness and Testimony*, novels about the Shoah demonstrate the possibility that "the language of fiction" may be "the best means that we have to approximate the heat of the fire itself," the actual event (81). Similarly, in a "postscript" to *In the Time of the Butterflies*, Julia Alvarez writes, "I wanted to immerse my readers in an epoch in the life of the Dominican Republic that I believe can only finally be understood by fiction, only finally be redeemed by the imagination. A novel is not, after all, a historical document, but a way to travel through the human heart" (324). Fiction may be the only way to heal the wounds left after the trujillato. Once Trujillo "was a bad memory in our past," Patria believes, "that would be the real revolution we would have to fight: forgiving each other for what we had let come to pass" (222). Ultimately, Alvarez ends the story of the girls' lives with the lesson of the novel and what it stands for. On the last day of the sisters' lives, as they finish their visit to their husbands in prison, they "said our hurried goodbyes, our whispered prayers and endearments. Remember . . . Don't forget" (295). Such is the function of Alvarez's historical novels of the Dominican Republic. It is only finally through fiction that the narratives of the island's history can be transformed into the Dominican people's collective memory. ⌒

CROSSING BORDERS AND WRITING MESTIZAJE

Negotiating Genre and Gender

Latina writing in the United States has been much lauded for generic border-crossing, a tradition that is apparent throughout the whole of Alvarez's work. In her exploration of Dominican collective memory, she calls attention to traditional divisions between history and fiction. In her writings of women in exile, she brings together fiction and autobiography. The border between these two genres limits Alvarez's ability to create multiple histories, fictions, and memories across the expanse of her narrative space, and she thus erases that border in order to engage in what she calls "making up the past" (*Other Side* 55). By making it up, rather than merely writing history or autobiography, Alvarez moves beyond traditional paradigms of fiction, history, memoir, and poetry. She not only draws different genres together, but she also innovates new forms of existing genres. This approach to her writing emerges out of her desire to create her own world in literature, "a world formed of contradictions, clashes, cominglings—the gringa and the Dominican" (*Something* 173). In the world she renders in her writing, she resists the conflation of Latino/a identity into a single, hybrid signifier. By drawing together and including the myriad experiences, cultures, identities, nations, and communities of the Caribbean and the United States, Alvarez writes into being the mestizaje of her new place on the map.

Alvarez resists the paradigm of fragmentation that often characterizes descriptions and theories of Caribbean history and culture. Antonio Benítez-Rojo cautions against "reduc[ing] the Caribbean to the single factor of its instability" (27), echoing Franklin Knight's assertion that "we have got to break the views of the Caribbean as a series of balkanized zones of polyglot peoples, with polyglot tongues and polyglot ideas." Knight wants to project "a more unified image" of the Caribbean that incorporates "variegated" societies to demonstrate that they have "more in common than they have apart" (59). Although she demonstrates interest in what binds communities together, Alvarez refuses to "unify" the U.S. Caribbean experience when she insists on the dis-integration of identity for women in exile or when she creates a single story or voice for Dominican history.

Another method of exposing that dis-integration is through her work with multiple genres. Because mestizaje is not fragmentation but accumulation, Alvarez's accumulation of genres also serves as a means of transcending constraints imposed from the outside on her writing, her identity, and her narrative space. In "Undercover Poet," which appears in *The Woman I Kept to Myself*, she asserts that "Under the cover of novels, I write poems" (129), revealing the various genres in which she inscribes her narrative vision.[1] Lizabeth Paravisini and Barbara Webb believe that Caribbean women writers exist on the threshold "between existing structures that tie us to the past and the need to define a different future" (106). One such structure that binds women writers to the past is genre, as they have been forced into paradigms codified and accepted by male writers in the European tradition. By deviating from those codified norms, Alvarez and other women writers with increasing access to publication can move toward defining the different future that Paravisini and Webb imagine.

The notion of women's crossing generic borders is not unique to Julia Alvarez.[2] Many feminist critics have pointed out that for women to write at all, they are transgressing both literary and gender boundaries by breaking the silence mandated for women. Deidre Lashgari finds that "[t]his double bind is especially strong for women of color, especially if their vision is shaped by a language other than English" (2). Several literary critics have noted generic transgression in Alvarez's novels, often in the context of the dynamics of race, nation, and language. Jacqueline

Stefanko, for example, in writing about *How the García Girls Lost Their Accents* has argued that

> [b]y purposefully fictionalizing her own historical, autobiographical life story in a polyphonic novel, Alvarez creates a new way of telling that crosses the boundaries between genres, between individual and community, between national identifications, and between continuity and disruption, giving definition to her writing as diasporic articulation. (56)

Stefanko's conception of Alvarez's boundary crossing is relevant for her writings because it begins to elucidate Alvarez's resistance to constraints on her narrative space. However, the notion of borders and transgression fails to account for Alvarez's project of inclusion as she draws into the space of the novel the multiplicity of the García girls' experiences, identities, and memories. Critics have noted genre transgression in *In the Time of the Butterflies* as well. Isabel Zakrzewski Brown sees Alvarez as, "in addition to a creator of fiction, [a] translator and interpreter given that the biographies and interviews she conducted were in Spanish" (100). Gus Puleo similarly sees *In the Time of the Butterflies* as a work that crosses genres, calling it a "novelized autobiographical chronicle in English" (13). Concepción Bados Ciria has also noted that Alvarez's "books cross borders with an obvious intention: to allay the pain of acculturation and the stigma of being an outsider by making the displacements of language and geography to be the medium of art" (406). Brown and Puleo seem to be moving toward the notion of accumulation in their descriptions, an accumulation that Alvarez writes in order to escape labels such as Ciria's "outsider."

The discussion of generic border crossing has led to larger questions of Alvarez's own "genre" as a writer. Elizabeth Coonrod Martínez, for example, suggests that Alvarez's work is "more Latin American than U.S.-exile writing" (264). Assessments like these emphasize Ralph Cohen's point in "History and Genre" that genre is historically contingent (204).

For Alvarez, genre is culturally contingent as well; her writing gathers the experiences, histories, literatures, languages, and cultures of the Caribbean and the United States, and she highlights gender in the mestizaje of her writing to demonstrate the intersections among these dimensions of experience. In Tzvetan Todorov's frequently cited etiology of genres, he writes that "[a] new genre is always a transformation of an earlier one, or of several: by inversion, by displacement, by combination" (15). Alvarez performs these transformations across the whole of her work, writing mestizaje in her novels for adults and children, her essays, and her poetry. Most of the critical attention to Alvarez's work has focused on her adult novels, primarily *How the García Girls Lost Their Accents, In the Time of the Butterflies*, and to a lesser extent, *¡Yo!* I want to make clear that Alvarez's project of mestizaje extends beyond her fiction to the other genres she uses to map the space she seeks to create. She moves beyond merely rendering her fiction "historical" or "autobiographical" to creating multiplicity both across and within genres.

MESTIZAJE ACROSS GENRES

For Alvarez, one important means of writing mestizaje is to address similar themes, topics, and experiences in a variety of genres. Alvarez first claimed her writer's voice and identity through poetry, although she had difficulty publishing her work until the release of *Homecoming* in 1984. "I wanted to write," she notes in "Have Typewriter, Will Travel," "but nobody would pay me to do it" (*Something* 181). She traveled throughout the United States, from Kentucky to California, teaching poetry writing workshops in schools, public libraries, and nursing homes. After a few publications in small poetry magazines, she began to take semester-long writer-in-residence jobs at universities all over the country, ending up with eighteen addresses in fifteen years (179). It is not surprising that many of the themes that permeate her fiction and essays—exile, displacement, language, creativity, memory, and womanhood—emerge first in her poetry. Her desire to "make up the past" can be traced throughout the poems of *Homecoming, The Other Side/El*

Otro Lado, and *The Woman I Kept to Myself.* In this later collection, Alvarez identifies her "current incarnation: ¡Latina poet!" (147).

As she developed her poetic voice, Alvarez doubted her choice of subject matter, believing that poetry should be reserved for topics "Important and Deep that would impress my readers. My voice in a poem should carry authority and weight as I spoke about the big matters that Milton, Yeats, Homer tackled" (*Something* 147). Alvarez's own memories play a role in her gradual understanding of the poetic value of her experiences. She says in an interview that, when writing the "Housekeeping" poems,[3]

> I was expecting to hear "Sing to me, muse, and through me tell the story." But when I closed my eyes what I heard were things like, Don't put so much vinegar in the lettuce, you are going to ruin the salad. You call that a blind stitch? I can't see it. This is the way you make a cake. I heard women talking to me about taking care of a house. That was what I heard growing up, voices of women doing things together in a household. (25)

She also discovered that the Chicana writers of the 1970s and, as she has repeatedly pointed out, Maxine Hong Kingston in *Woman Warrior* were writing their own lives. Alvarez ultimately recognized how the rigid division between women's experience and the masculine literary tradition of poetry was detrimental to women writers. She then set about "claiming my woman's voice" (*Homecoming* 119). The themes that she develops in her poetry are distillations of her experiences of displacement and loss, explorations of the U.S. Caribbean writer's life in exile. The poetic voice that emerges in *Homecoming, The Other Side/El Otro Lado,* and *The Woman I Kept to Myself* is Alvarez's own; the distance between Alvarez and the narrator of her poems is narrow.

The subject matter of her poetry reflects the woman's voice that Alvarez claims and carries through to her other writings, creating parallel stories in different genres that reveal multiple dimensions and perspectives of the same events. Gladys, the maid in "The Gladys Poems" in *The Other Side/El Otro Lado*, worked for the Alvarez family in the Dominican Republic; she is, Alvarez admits in *Something to Declare*, the object of "my deepest identification" (154). Gladys "was the pantry maid, light-skinned and pretty, with a beautiful voice and a repertoire of songs, many of them Mexican mariachi songs, which she taught me to sing" (154). A muse for Alvarez, Gladys appears in "The Gladys Poems" as "Gladys Singing." "*Singing*, she told me, *makes/ everything else possible*" (10), a lesson Alvarez learns in her own writing. Alvarez's child-voice in the Gladys poems laments her loss as well, wondering "Gladys, where did you go?" in her poem "Abandoned." The child only knows that "In hushed whispers I heard/ that your fingers had been picking/ our absent-minded pockets./ Another version ran/ that an uncle's eye had been caught/ roving by a jealous aunt" (20). From these conflicting stories emerges Alvarez's task of presenting multiple stories from several perspectives, creating a world in which there is no single identifiable Truth and women's lives remain full of possibilities.

The maid from "The Gladys Poems" also appears in *How the García Girls Lost Their Accents*. In the chapter "An American Surprise," which is narrated by Carla, Gladys is dismissed from the family's employ as was the Gladys of "Gladys Singing." In this expanded scene, Carla has given Gladys a music box that her grandparents had purchased for Carla in the United States. When it is discovered in Gladys's room, the maid leaves the house, "dabbing at her eyes with another kerchief" (273). When Carla begs her father not to send Gladys away, he tells her, "It was Gladys who asked to leave, you know . . ." (273), ending with a pause that suggests the story might not be true. Alvarez returns to this character and this scene over and over again in her poetry, her personal essays, and her fiction, pointing to her desire to fill in gaps in her own knowledge and memory, to make up (for) the past. Her effort to rework this material repeatedly suggests her desire to escape the limits of a single story, even in her own work.[4] She seeks through diverse stories, spaces, and genres to undermine the official story that has dominated her Dominican history and collective memory.

Alvarez explores the process of recreating lost or missing memories in "Making Up the Past," a poem that appears in *The Other Side/El Otro Lado*. She adumbrates the losses of memory to exile, displacement, time, and change. She laments, "This never happened and yet I want the memory/ so much I have made it true" (55), which drives her recreation of her own life (through the García girls) and of women in Dominican history (the Mirabal sisters and Salomé Ureña and Camila Henríquez). In "Making Up the Past," Alvarez improvises a memory:

> The memory or rather pseudo memory
> is of my mother in a bathrobe at the window
> watching my progress down the block
> and around the corner until I am out of sight,
> not knowing (how could she know?)
> and knowing (she always knows everything!)
> of my terror at setting off by myself
> to Hillside to pick up something she needs. (56)

The adult Alvarez realizes that her mother's bathrobe is "a flowered bathrobe/ she never owned," but she makes it her mother's by adding a "zipper fixed twice already/ from my mother's roughhandling/ (always in a hurry)" (57), details that permit Alvarez to claim the bathrobe and the memory for her own. This scene is "how my memory ends childhood" (56), as Alvarez becomes lost on her way to the store, a terrifying experience that she explores in regard to her lost childhood, her lost homeland, and her lost memories. Even today, the adult Alvarez writes, "I can make myself feel lost all over again,/ feel that thirty years have passed in which all I've been doing is reading street signs/ for a way back to a moment that never/ (I am sure of it) never happened" (57–58).

For Alvarez, however, that past moment of loss is present; she still finds herself "adrift in America" (56), as the child lost in her new land feels not only in her new neighborhood but also in her new language, her new culture, her new identity as Dominican and American. Rather than risk losing memory and cultural identity altogether, she is compelled to create "this movie we must make of the past/ so that it doesn't break our hearts/ or worse, leave us, in remembering it,/ leaves, untouched and dismissive" (58). Alvarez reveals in these lines that forgetting is the worst pain of memory, and she thus transforms her efforts in "making up the past" into the creative power of improvisation. In her memory, the child Alvarez walks down the block,

> my shoulders already set
> in a posture I assume every time
> I sit down to write—a feisty, terrified squaring
> of the shoulders—my hands fisting
> in my pockets and all of me refusing
> (for the moment) to turn back and face
> what I am leaving behind, what I must know
> I will keep coming back to all my imagined life. (58)

Alvarez's imagined life reappears throughout her work, much of it centering on what she left behind as an exile and as a child coming to the United States from the Dominican Republic. She recognizes that those losses are precisely at "the center of my art" (*García Girls* 290), drawn repeatedly in her efforts to recreate stories absent in her memory.

The poem "Exile" in *The Other Side/El Otro Lado* reveals the same attempt to work out the relationship between lost memories and her writing. Alvarez has no memory of what happened the day she left the island, yet she has to imagine it for the García girls in *How the García Girls Lost Their Accents*. Although she admits in *Something to Declare* her inability to remember what she sees as the pivotal event of her life, she reenvisions the memory for herself in the poem "Exile." Her father tells the girls they are going to the beach, and Alvarez takes up the metaphor of water as the medium through which their exile begins, blurring her memory and slowing the pace of the poem. Leaving the house "we wouldn't see again for another decade,/ I let myself lie back in the deep waters," allowing herself to float out, "past the driveway, past the gates,/ in the black Ford, Papi grim at the wheel,/ winding through back roads, stroke by difficult stroke,/ out on the highway, heading toward the coast" (*Other Side* 26). When they pass the road for the family's beach house, the sisters protest, and their parents reassure them that "there was a better surprise in store for us!" (26). Although her sisters do not suspect their flight from the country, the child Julia has "already swum up ahead and guessed/ some loss larger than I understood" (26). Throughout the night, "in a fitful sleep, I swam," and climbing aboard the airplane, their family "had been set adrift" (27), the same metaphor Alvarez uses in "Making Up the Past," after the family has been in the United States for three years. Adrift as exiles in the United States, she and her Papi are "two swimmers looking down/ at the quiet surface of our island waters,/ seeing their faces right before plunging in,/ eager, afraid, not yet sure of the outcome" (28). That Alvarez returns repeatedly to this event, and to the resulting condition of exile, demonstrates that she is yet exploring the outcome of exile, displacement, and loss.

The return to these same experiences points to Alvarez's use of a variety of genres to engage in what Leigh Gilmore has called "autobiographics." Autobiographics is a set of practices—"those elements of self-representation"—that "mark a location in a text where self-invention, self-discovery, and self-representation emerge within the technologies of autobiography" (42). Rather than "a kind of genre per se," autobiographics as Gilmore conceives it is "a kind of writing," a conception that emphasizes "the extent to which women's autobiography invades, permeates, and also is invaded by canonical genres" (41). This notion of autobiography's invading and being invaded by canonical genres points to women writers' insistence on crossing traditional generic boundaries in their writings, efforts at resisting the myriad constraints on their lives and identities. What is useful about Gilmore's theory of autobiographics for Alvarez's writings is that it reveals representation, discovery, and, most important, invention to be at the heart of Alvarez's accumulating genres. It also allows us to conceive of her "historical fiction"—the stories of the Mirabal sisters and of Salomé Ureña—as a kind of biographics, a set of practices in which Alvarez invents, discovers, and represents these historical figures in her novels. Moreover, through the lens of auto/biographics—both her telling of her own story and that of the Mirabal sisters and the Ureña women through fiction—Alvarez explores her own experience of exile through the story of Camila Henríquez; she also creates parallels between her own commitment to break the silence imposed by Trujillo in order to resist tyranny and Minerva Mirabal's struggle with tyranny. Although Gilmore calls autobiographics "a discursive hybrid," recapitulating the dominance of hybridity, I would suggest instead that these practices are multiple and myriad and do not combine or fuse, but rather accumulate throughout all of Alvarez's work as well as within the individual books.

Alvarez's essays, fiction, and poetry thus reveal her own autobiographics. The essays in *Something to Declare* resonate with the events of her fiction and poetry. The events of her life that she describes in her essays about their arrival in the United States—"Our Papers," "My English," and "La Gringuita"—appear throughout *How the García Girls Lost Their Accents*. She suggests in an interview that "[a] lot of *The García Girls* was based on my own experience—first novels usually are. But there is a lot of fictionalizing, using the material of your life but being primarily interested in making a good story. It's the combining, the exaggeration, the redoing, the adding on, that makes it original rather than autobiographical" (Rosario-Sievert 35). There is so much of her experience in her fiction, in fact, that she has made textual changes to her novels to avoid libel charges, "tak[ing] drinks out of characters' hands and mak[ing] abused ladies disabused and mak[ing] so many changes in hair coloring and hairstyle that I could start a literary beauty parlor" (*Something* 274). She writes in *Something to Declare*:

> Indeed like any small tribe my familia has its national literature:
> the family stories. And, of course, so much of my material has

been inspired by these stories. I don't mean that my fiction recounts "what actually happened," but that my sense of the world, and therefore of the world I re-create in language, comes from that first encompassing experience of familia with its large cast of colorful characters, its elaborate branchings hither and yon to connect everyone together, its Babel of voices. (125–26)

By drawing parallels between her family stories and national literature, Alvarez blurs the lines between the personal and the public and between family and nation. These artificial divisions have no place in Alvarez's work in which she also effaces the line between the imaginary and "what actually happened." "In my familia," she writes, "fiction is a form of fact," and this "fictive cast of mind extends, of course, beyond families and small communities to politics and government and the wider culture" (124). She cites Trujillo's efforts to create the fiction of the Dominican Republic as a white nation and as a democracy, reinforcing her own efforts to present the Truth in her fiction—particularly about the trujillato—beyond factual occurrences and events.

Alvarez renders such Truths not only in her adult fiction but in her fiction for young readers as well. Caribbean writer Thelma Perkins points out the importance of writing for and about children when she asserts that writers must counter what she sees as "a legacy of silence" (106). She claims that Caribbean writers "owe our children their history" because "the future depends on our history and the way we interpret it" (106). By inscribing her experiences in narratives for children and young adults, Alvarez hopes to provide Caribbean children with the kinds of memories that she lost as a child under Trujillo and in exile.[5] Children's literature, according to Perry Nodelman, is a particularly appropriate place for such extensions. Children's books, he writes, are

short, simple, often didactic in intention, and clearly positive in their outlook on life—optimistic, with happy endings. But second, as the extensive critical discussion of many of these texts

implies, their apparent simplicity contains depths, often surprisingly pessimistic qualifications of the apparent optimism,
dangerously and delightfully counterproductive possibilities
that oppose and undermine the apparent messages. (1–2)

Some of the best children's literature, Nodelman notes, "expresses itself
most often in terms of describing meetings and interminglings of
things that are seen, by us and by the narrator and the characters, as
belonging in different or even opposite categories" (9). Individually,
Alvarez's books draw on these interminglings—the mestizaje of the
Caribbean—to write the immigrant experience in *How Tía Lola Came
to ~~Visit~~ Stay* and the Dominican experience under Trujillo in *Before We
Were Free*. In a broad sense, Alvarez's locating of the terrors of the trujillato and the subsequent *ajusticiamiento,* as she does in *Before We Were
Free*, in a book for children affirms the seeming opposition that
Nodelman describes. But aside from the obvious fact that thousands of
children suffered under the trujillato and after the ajusticiamiento, the
apparent simplicity of the genre of children's literature allows Alvarez
to extend the purpose and force of the testimonio of that history and to
celebrate the power of the voice—even for children.

As in her adult novels, Alvarez emphasizes in *Before We Were Free*
the way Trujillo constructed his own fiction of both the country and of
himself. To share with young readers the realities of life under Trujillo
in the Dominican Republic, Alvarez writes the details of the regime in
the novel. Anita de la Torre explains that Trujillo's "picture hangs in our
front entryway with the saying below it: IN THIS HOUSE, TRUJILLO RULES"
(19–20). She remarks that "[e]veryone had always treated El Jefe like
God. I shudder to think how many times I've prayed to him instead of
to Jesus on His cross" (48). Such glorification is not surprising consid-
ering scenes such as the life-sized Nativity "set up on the lawn below the
towering statue of El Jefe on his horse. It looks as if those shepherds and
camels and even Mary and Joseph have come all the way from
Bethlehem just to see him" (38). Anita comes to understand the terrors

of her country; although she wants to believe Trujillo's fiction that Dominicans are free, Anita thinks "about how the SIM raided our property, how Tío Toni had to disappear, how I have to erase everything in my diary," and she realizes the truth: "We're *not* free—we're trapped" (48). After Trujillo's assassination, Anita and her mother are forced to hide in the walk-in closet of the Italian counsel general because of her father's role in the plot. Ultimately, she and her mother follow her sister to safety in the United States, leaving behind "a quilt of faces and memories spreading out over the sea" (142).

Alvarez draws on her own memories of exile as she describes Anita's arrival in the United States. When Anita attends a new school in New York City, her teacher points out the Dominican Republic to the class. Anita realizes, "[t]o them, it's just a geography lesson; to me, it's home" (144). Being considered a geography lesson resonates with a scene from *How the García Girls Lost Their Accents*, in which Yolanda García dates a young man whose parents treat her "like a geography lesson for their son" as well (98). Although too young to date, Anita has had a variety of friends from different places—Italy, the United States, the Dominican Republic—who have given her the ability to see her various worlds from different perspectives. With such hard-won maturity, Anita ironically doubts, even in the United States, whether she lives in a free country. Perhaps, she wonders, the United States "is a free country only for Americans" (*Before* 149). What Alvarez offers in this novel for young readers is the means for dealing with terror, displacement, and loss, the same means that Yolanda García chooses and the same means that Alvarez herself has chosen—writing. "Only writing in my diary helps me feel a little less crazy," Anita writes (46), discovering that "[b]efore I wrote all this out, I didn't really know I felt this way deep down" (42). Alvarez offers writing—and erasing—as a means of not only expressing the loss but of exploring it and understanding it, both in the Dominican Republic and the United States. Consonant with Alvarez's writings, Anita's diary serves as the material accumulation of those thoughts and events in a narrative space—the multiplicity, not the hybrid unity, of the postcolonial experience. The narrative space of her diary functions as a microcosm of Alvarez's entire oeuvre in its representation and accumulation of Dominican and North American histories, memories, and identities.

Alvarez's book for middle-grade readers, *How Tía Lola Came to ~~Visit~~ Stay*, takes up the same issues. Nine-year-old Miguel Guzman has moved from New York City to Vermont, where he encounters not only the conflation of Latino/a identity but of all ethnic identity. In Vermont, Miguel's "black hair and brown skin stand out. He feels so different from everybody. 'Are you Indian?' one kid asks him, impressed," and Miguel has to explain to his classmates, "We're Latinos" (5). But during a visit to the Dominican Republic, Miguel "wonders what makes him a real American. Because he was born in New York—unlike his parents who were both born in the Dominican Republic? Because he speaks English? Because his favorite baseball team is the Yankees? Because he still likes hot dogs more than *arroz con habichuelas*?" (133). The cultural trappings of identity—language, games, food—coexist with geography as a determinant of identity, and Miguel does not know which dimension of his experience takes primacy in self-definition. Through Miguel's younger sister, Juanita, Alvarez further explores the generational differences between those who immigrate to the United States and their children who are born there. On a visit to the Dominican Republic, Juanita wonders, "So, was that their home?" and remains uncertain about "where she is from. Both her mami and her papi came from the Dominican Republic. She was born in New York and lived there all her life until eight months ago, when they moved to Vermont. So is she from Vermont now?" (121). Confused by her displacement, "Juanita feels lost when she thinks of all the places she is from. Maybe she will never know where she really, *really* belongs" (122). Alvarez thus situates this novel in a long tradition of immigrant literature and reveals her own connection to that literary tradition in the United States.

In Vermont, Miguel feels his displacement even more acutely with the arrival of his Tía Lola from the Dominican Republic. She looks different, talks differently, and acts differently than everyone else in Vermont, and he feels embarrassed by her colorful clothes and mannerisms. As he gets to know her, however, "Miguel has to admit there is one totally fun thing about Tía Lola. She tells great stories" (17). Storytelling becomes Tía Lola's primary function in the novel and the means by which Miguel comes to explore and understand his displacement as a Dominican American in Vermont. Storytelling also permits Alvarez to reunite the divergence of truth and fiction, drawing the two together into the narrative space of the book. Miguel notes, "None of Tía Lola's stories sound exactly true, but Miguel doesn't care. While he listens, he feels as if he isn't in Vermont at all, but in a magical world where anything can happen" (17). That magical world is part of Alvarez's new geography, which she herself enacts through these kinds of stories. Through these stories, Miguel and Juanita find the link to home that they thought they were missing, which their mother points out to them. It's important, she tells them, "that you hear Tía Lola's stories so you can always stay connected to your past" (118–19). Alvarez draws parallels between distance in time and in space through her use of multiple generations and multiple locations, brought together into the space of the novel. When Juanita understands that she really belongs with her family, Alvarez is presenting to her young readers another means of dealing with displacement—family connections made visible through storytelling—the same strategy Alvarez herself is using in the writing of this novel and her others.

Mestizaje Within Genres

Another of her children's books demonstrates not only the way that Alvarez writes across genres, drawing on the same subject matter—the United States and the Dominican Republic—but also the way she draws different genres into the children's story to create an accumulation of genres rather than an accumulation of themes.[6] *A Cafecito Story* is the tale of Joe, "a gringo going on forty" (9), who is something of "a young radical" in his home state of Nebraska because he "liked reading more than football" (26). A schoolteacher and son of a farmer, Joe is disillusioned with his life and decides to take a trip to one of those islands he has seen in glossy travel brochures. Disappointed with the Dominican resort experience, he travels into the mountains at the recommendation of a roadside coffee vendor. In the course of Joe's trip, he befriends the locals and decides to quit his job in Nebraska and buy a coffee farm in the Dominican Republic after hearing how "his small farmer neighbors are about to cave in and rent their plots and grow coffee for [a corporation] using the new techniques" (15), which will destroy the environment. After fifteen years of farming coffee in the Dominican Republic, Joe returns to Nebraska for a brief visit, where he meets a waitress who loves to read and harbors a long-held dream to be a writer. They marry, and he exhorts her to write the story of coffee, which is ostensibly *A Cafecito Story*. Alvarez brings into this little coffee story ecology, agriculture, politics, education, and the economic intricacies of fair trade practices.

Alvarez effects the didacticism that Nodelman identified as common to children's literature through lessons rendered in story. For "the story of coffee," Alvarez explains the growth process from germination to harvest and from drying to bagging. She sets out the economics and politics of coffee growing, contrasting corporate practices to local farming techniques. Joe's friend Miguel is tempted to work for *la compañía* because "[i]f we work for them we will get 80 pesos a day, 150 if we are willing to spray the poison. I get 35 pesos for a caja of beans, Carmen can pick two cajas a day. It takes three years for me to get a coffee harvest. On a plantation, with their sprays, they have coffee in a year" (17). Alvarez also presents, after the story, a lesson for adults in fair trade, which "guarantees farmers like Carmen and Miguel" direct sales for their cooperatives, a fair price, improved access to credit, marketing, and a commitment from buyers to support environmental sustainability (47). This section of the book is clearly written for adults; the vocabulary and syntax are more sophisticated, and there is no narrative with which to teach the intended lesson. The final section of the book provides names, addresses, and descriptions of fourteen resources for fair-trade coffee and cooperative organizations. These different sections demonstrate not only Alvarez's efforts to instruct but also her insistence on the multiplicity of genres in the telling of a story. She transforms the genre of "children's fiction" into a multidisciplinary look at the coffee industry and farming practices in the Dominican Republic and the United States.

Because the story is one for "children of all ages," the book simplifies the economic and political situation of the Dominican farmers and thus tends toward idealization. Joe observes that "Miguel's house is made of pinewood, and the roof is zinc, the door is opened. There were no electric wires, no telephone poles. Miguel smiles in welcome, half a dozen kids around him. Carmen, his wife, is out back, boiling *rábanos* for their supper" (13). Alvarez presents the lack of electricity and telecommunications as an advantage of the rural life, romanticizing the simplicity of the small family farm. None of the campesinos can read or write, and part of Joe's mission as school-teacher-turned-farmer is to teach them to read. Intellectual, economic, and even moral growth parallels the growth of the crop. Joe observes that

> [b]y the time Miguel and Carmen and their children have learned to write their names, the little seeds have sprouted. When the trees are a foot high, the family has struggled through a sentence. All of them can read a page by the time the trees reach up to Miguel's knees. When the coffee is as tall as little Miguelina, they have progressed to chapters. In three years, by the time of the first coffee harvest from trees Joe has planted, Miguel and Carmen and their children can read a whole book. (24–25)

Alvarez overtly connects these two phenomena when she writes that "[t]he world can only be saved by one man or woman putting a seed in the ground or a story in someone's head or a book in someone's hands" (37). Storytelling, as all of Alvarez's work attests, is both transformative and salvific.

In one of the poems in *Homecoming*, Alvarez also draws together seemingly antithetical genres into a single work. Mixing an alphabet primer with the violent political history of the world, Alvarez teaches her readers a new geography of terror and tragedy. Suggesting that her English-speaking audience of the United States needs instruction in the widespread political crimes in history, Alvarez uses a children's genre to address adult concerns. In this "modern primer for our kids," Alvarez writes,

> A is for Auschwitz; B for Biafra;
> Chile, Dachau; El Salvador; F is
> the Faulklands; Grenada; Hiroshima
> stands for H; Northern Ireland for I;
> J is for Jonestown; K for Korea;
> L for massacres in Lidice; My Lai;
> N, Nicaragua; O, Okinawa;
> P is the Persian Gulf and Qatar, Q;
> Rwanda; Sarajevo—this year's hell;
> T is Treblinka and Uganda U;
> Vietnam and Wounded Knee. What's left to spell?
> An X to name the countless disappeared
> when they are dust in Yemen or Zaire. (72)

Not only does this primer elucidate the geography of death that characterized the twentieth century, it also emphasizes Alvarez's insistence on the primary roles of language and memory in our conception of that history. This poem serves not only to teach but also to remember—and to make others remember—the violence of the last century. And she approaches this memory through language at its most elemental level, the alphabet. Recognizing that these disasters occurred and knowing the names of these geographical locations are only the beginning of the project; we must learn their histories as well. By using the primer frame for the lessons, Alvarez highlights the childlike oblivion of U.S. readers to the world's geography and history.

Alvarez also draws genres together in her novel *In The Name of Salomé*. She titles each chapter after a poem by Salomé Ureña, coupling the title in Spanish for Salomé's chapters with its English translation for

Camila's chapters. She thus ties together inversely the stories of Salomé and Camila. The first chapter is titled "El Ave y el nido," and tells the story of the beginning of Salomé's life; this chapter is coupled with "Bird and Nest," the story of the later years of Camila's life. "Luz," the Spanish counterpart to "Light," appears as the final chapter of Salomé's life, just before her death in 1894. By using these titles to frame the story—"El ave y el nido," "Contestación," "La fe en el porvenir," "Amor y anhelo," "Sombras," "Ruinas," "La llegada del invierno," and "Luz"—Alvarez draws Ureña's actual writings into the novel, and the themes of her life become the themes of Alvarez's work as well. Seeing her patria in ruins, Ureña laments, "¡Oh mi Antilla infeliz que el alma adora!" (95). [Oh, my unhappy island that my soul worships!] Alvarez draws on this "unhappiness" in Dominican history to present that history to another audience. When Ureña envisions the "Luz" that awaits her country, she writes,

> Es esa la futura
> prenda de paz, de amor y de grandeza,
> la que el bien de los pueblos asegura,
> la base de firmeza
> donde al mundo, con timbres y blasones,
> se elevan prepotentes las naciones. (142)
> [It is the future
> pledged to peace, to love and to greatness,
> which the goodness of its peoples assures,
> the stable foundation
> on which, with great ringing and glory, to the world
> the powerful nations reach.]

Alvarez uses this "Light" to illuminate the birth of Camila, who will secure the future for Salomé and for the Dominican Republic. Camila does so by returning to Cuba at the end of her life to "build the kind of country [her mother] dreamed of" (*In the Name* 335), and to fight for a patria in which she wholly believes. Although Camila believes Pedro to be her mother's favorite and the recipient of her mother's gift, Salomé's poetry and Dominican history are the "Luz" of Alvarez's novel. For Camila's part, her motivation to "struggle to create the country we dream of" stems from Salomé's dream to "make a patria out of the land beneath our feet. That much I learned from my mother" (350). Through Ureña's poetry, Alvarez illuminates the novel, drawing not only two genres together but also two writers, two epochs, and two histories.

THE MESTIZAJE OF WOMEN'S CREATIVITY

In the same way that she draws different genres together in her poetry, in her children's books, and in her adult novels, Alvarez also draws different forms of creativity together, revealing correlations to writing. Because Alvarez's narrative space is characterized by mestizaje, she improvises those correlations across activities. She demonstrates, for example, the processes of housekeeping and cooking as tantamount to writing. These tasks are gendered, revealing Alvarez's belief in women's improvisatory power to create in every dimension of their lives. Moreover, she suggests that women negotiate a number of identities—housekeeper, mother, artist, writer, and cook—that coexist simultaneously. While society exerts cultural pressure to condense those identities into a single, dominant one, such as Stay-at-Home-Mom or Artist, Alvarez recognizes that women can be both simultaneously—and many others. The multiplicity of these identities resonates in the multiplicity of activities—different genres of artistic expression—that emerge in Alvarez's writings.

Homecoming, which was originally published in 1984, was re-released in 1996 after Alvarez's successes with *How the García Girls Lost Their Accents* and *In the Time of the Butterflies*. The twelve-year gap between editions allowed Alvarez to reexamine her previous work from a different perspective, and she describes the younger poet's language in the Afterword to the 1996 edition of the book. *Homecoming* is the book "where I started: in these poems I claimed my woman's legacy and my vocation as a writer" (120). In order to claim her voice as a woman and a writer, Alvarez searched the models of her childhood and found that "[t]he only models I had been given by my mother and aunts and the heroines of novels were the homemaking model and the romantic model" (118). Ultimately, "[a]s I followed my mother cleaning house, washing and ironing clothes, rolling dough, I was using the material of my housebound girl life to claim my woman's legacy" (119). Writing about these household tasks also provides Alvarez with a means of collecting and organizing her own memories, a personal "housekeeping" that permits her to write the legacy that led her to move out of the "housebound girl life" and assert the diversity of her Dominican American woman writer's life.

While her poetry reveals the ways she has transformed homemaking into writing in the creation of her identity, her poems also expose the difficulty of that process. Alvarez's voice as a young poet strongly disdains homemaking when she sees it as her mother has lived it. In "Dusting," the child Alvarez writes her name in the dust accumulated on the furniture just before her mother comes by with a cloth, and the words she inscribes on those objects speak to Alvarez's resistance: "But I refused with every mark/ to be like her, anonymous" (9). Such work is unrecognized as are those who perform it. She sees her mother's invisibility in the craft of sewing as well. In "New Clothes," she writes that her mother's craft was "more perfect in invisibility/ her outfits successes when they looked/ as if she hadn't made them" (32). As we see in Anita's diary in *Before We Were Free*, this invisibility—this erasure of self—is complex; while Anita silences herself as an act of rebellion against Trujillo by keeping her own secrets, the erasure of Alvarez's mother in her creative acts force her to risk her own identity as an artist. The young Alvarez in the poem sees the erasure of her mother's identity in all of these acts of house cleaning, writing in "Mother Love," "The house gleamed clean as if it'd been ransacked/ of all the fantasies which she denied" (44). Alvarez enacts her desire to escape her mother's life, wishing desperately in "Storm Windows" to climb the "ladder/ she had forbidden me" to use while they wash the storm windows of the house:

I wanted to mount that ladder,
rung by rung, look down [...]
I wanted to rise, polishing into each pane
another section of the sky.
Then give a kick, unbuckling
her hands clasped about my ankles,
and sail up, beyond her reach,
her house, her yard, her mothering. (18)

The young Alvarez believes that she must necessarily repudiate house-keeping and even mothering, as these are the things that tie women to the ground and render them unable to rise into the sky beyond the reach of responsibilities and lost fantasies.

There are glimpses in the "Housekeeping" poems that the young poet Alvarez is beginning to recognize the connections between such work and her own art. An accomplished seamstress, her mother can "unroll the bolts and name/ the fabric from which our clothing came,/ dress the world in vocabulary" (34), the same task as the writer's. In the final poem of the "Housekeeping" section of *Homecoming*, Alvarez writes "Woman's Work," in which she asks, "Who says a woman's work isn't high art?" It is not only high art, she suggests, but "a hard art." Finally, Alvarez concludes that "Her woman's work was nothing less than art" (45). This repetition of the equivalence of housework to art work points to Alvarez's drawing together of traditional woman's work and her own work, multiple facets of women's creativity.

Another model of women's creativity comes from Alvarez's Tía Titi, whom Alvarez describes in the essay "Of Maids and Other Muses." As "a very different kind of aunt" than the other models available to her, Tía Titi "sat by herself on the couch with her legs tucked under her, reading a book. You asked her what a word meant, and she knew what it meant and a number of other things about that word as well. We were not sup-posed to mention that she was a jamona, an old maid" (*Something* 150). Titi, however, did not want to get married; "[i]nstead, she focused on her books and her beautiful garden" (151). Alvarez had earlier examined the model of Tía Tití in the "Housekeeping" poem "Orchids," the longest poem in the collection at 150 lines. As she is called in the poem, Tía Chica (Aunt Girl or Aunt Small) "would never marry" (*Homecoming* 37). She had no interest in marrying, and she had her own garden, which makes her eligible for entrance into the male-dominated orchid society. "The men of the Orchid Society" arrive to measure and define, coming back "astonished,/ wiping their creased foreheads: 'Twenty-two varieties! The work of a single woman!'" (38–39). Alvarez plays on the sobriquet "single woman" to point out what her aunt had accomplished on her own as well as her aunt's relative freedom as a single woman without the duties of a wife and mother.

In "Orchids," Tía Chica does not remain a single woman, marrying in her thirties and gaining a husband as well as housekeeping tasks, which Alvarez associates with marriage and motherhood. When the poet visits her Tía Chica in New York City where she lives with her husband, Tía Chica "remembered, she said, the orchids,/ they were a good diversion,/ though twenty-two varieties/ were hard work for a single woman" (*Homecoming* 40). Calling the orchids a diversion suggests Chica's adoption of dominant cultural values about women's obligation to marry. Because she is no longer a single woman, her aunt no longer raises orchids. Instead,

> the children must be raised,
> the piano cover lifted,
> the metronome beat seconded
> with the nods of a proud mother.
> The husband too has his stories
> and needs the "ah" of a listener
> who has never heard such wonders.
> The grandfather must be wiped
> when he dribbles like a newborn. (41)

These duties keep her aunt from her own work, and Alvarez, by dedicating "Orchids" to the memory of her aunt and her flowers, pays homage to women who are not wives and mothers. As Tía Chica enumerates what Alvarez sees as the real diversions from her aunt's true art, Alvarez writes,

> But I celebrate for a moment
> the single-minded labors
> of the single woman artist:
> the widow squeezes the whey
> through the cheesecloth that she bunches,
> the shy nuns stitch their crosses
> on linens of the altar,
> the silly lacemakers knot
> a thousand complications
> as they giggle and they gossip. (41)

The women mentioned here are the women who have historically had the necessary freedom for their artistry—widows, nuns, and spinsters. Here she also hints at the artistic value in women's traditional labors in cheese making, lace making, and embroidery.

Paradoxically, while Alvarez sings the praises of the single woman artist, she also recognizes the collectivity of women's art, the community of women who often perform such labors. In "What Could It Be?" Alvarez celebrates her aunts as they cook together:

> Around the kettle of chicken and rice,
> the aunts were debating what flavor was missing.
> Tía Carmen guessed garlic.
> Tía Rosa, some coarsely ground pepper.
> Tía Ana, so tidy she wore the apron,
> shook her head, plain salt what was needed.
> Tía Fofi, afraid to be wrong, echoed salt.

Just a pinch, she apologized, reaching for the shaker.
Tía Gladys said parsley never hurt anything.
Tía Victoria frowned and pronounced,
Tarragon. No one disagreed. (29)

Alvarez values the variety of spices each woman brings to the kettle, and "[t]he aunts each put in a shake of their favorites" (29). The community of the aunts results not only in the celebration of their collective art but also in a meal that allows them to provide for their families. An older Alvarez concludes in her essay "On Maids and Other Muses" that "my voice would not be found up in a tower, in those upper reaches or important places, but down in the kitchen among the women who first taught me about service, about passion, about singing as if my life depended on it" (*Something* 162).

Alvarez's later writings continue to develop the connection between cooking and her art, demonstrating the way she expands her notion of genre—not just in literature but in activities. In the foreword to her husband's cookbook, *The New Family Cookbook: Recipes for Nourishing Yourself and Those You Love* (2000), Alvarez again acknowledges her "tías, cocineras, and a mami" who "might as well have been in Michelangelo's studio: they were creating works of art" ("How" xv–xvi). In an essay in the same book, she equates writing and cooking insofar as "style in cooking, as in writing, often does have to do with personal touch" (*New Family* 95). These lessons were not easy to learn; she once believed that she had to choose between being one of those women who cook or one of those women who write; however, "[a]s my own cooking repertoire expanded beyond brownies, I discovered the wonderful pleasure of transforming a pile of ingredients into a recipe that nurtured and sometimes delighted people I love. It was akin to writing a poem, after all" (*Something* 85). The mestizaje of ingredients that expanded her cooking repertoire parallel the mestizaje of her writing, both acts not only of creativity but also of transformation. Alvarez has recognized that as a writer, she is also a woman—with all that encompasses, including housekeeping and cooking if she so chooses. By valuing these activities, rather than seeing them as impossible to reconcile with her life as a writer, Alvarez expands the notion of woman's identity to include the myriad possibilities—not choices—for women's lives.

Alvarez's efforts at drawing together the aspects of her writing—genre, experience, identity, and activity—point to her response to the increasing fragmentation of not only Caribbean history, politics, and experience but also of the world. By rendering collective activities traditionally conceived as individual—housekeeping, cooking, writing—Alvarez further emphasizes the collectivity and variety of the U.S. Caribbean woman writer's experience. By insisting on revealing rather than collapsing Salomé Ureña's work in *In the Name of Salomé,* by bringing alive the muse and maid Gladys in poetry, nonfiction, and fiction, by writing for "children of all ages," Alvarez insists on the mestizaje of genre and gender that shape the life of the U.S. Caribbean woman writer. ⌒

MAGICAL THINKING

Syncretism, Spirituality, and Stories

Alvarez's new place on the map includes not only exile, improvisation, memory, and genre but also the religious and spiritual practices of the Caribbean. Early maps of Hispaniola reveal the centrality of religion to the colonial project. In the sixteenth, seventeenth, and even eighteenth centuries—before legends routinely appeared on maps of the Caribbean—mapmakers often marked towns with crosses or even tiny, stylized churches, which were sometimes scaled to indicate the size of the settlement. For the European readers of these maps, towns thus came into existence through the construction and then representation of a Catholic church. Absent from these maps are the practices of the indigenous peoples and the slaves the Europeans later forced to the region. Jesuit priest P.F.X. Charlevoix adds religion to his description of the peoples of the island, writing, "On ne devoit pas attendre un système de Religion bien sensé & bien suivi d'une Nation si brutte, si peu accountumée à réflechir, & si peu éclairée des lumieres même de la Raison naturelle" (70). [One must not expect a well-developed religious system from a nation of people so coarse, so little accustomed to reflection, and so unenlightened even by natural reason.] Because the indigenous people did not practice Catholicism, Charlevoix assumed the absence of any spiritual system. It is precisely these absences that Julia Alvarez is trying to presence—in Homi Bhabha's sense of the word[1]—on her own map of the Caribbean and the United States. The mestizaje of spirituality emerges in Alvarez's narrative space as she depicts not only the Catholicism of the Spanish but also the Santería and the Vodou[2] as they are practiced on the island.

Contemporary constructions of hybridity dominate no dimension of Caribbean theory more than the domain of spirituality and religion.

The belief systems of the Caribbean are frequently described as "syncretic," and much of the scholarship on the hybridity of the region has emerged out of the discussion of its religious traditions. Yet the concept of syncretism, like hybridity, threatens to erase the traditions that compose the syncretic. Alvarez seeks to inscribe the individual practices of a variety of religious systems that exist in the Dominican Republic. These systems emerged as a result of the region's colonial history. Alan Cambeira points out that in the "Great Encounter" between indigenous peoples and the invading Europeans, transculturation was not effected; instead, the invading Spanish culture "eventually destroy[ed] the indigenous militarily weaker one" (212). In the Caribbean, transculturation actually occurred not only between the indigenous peoples and the Spanish but also among the Spanish, the indios, and the slaves the Spanish imported from both Africa and Spain, creating such varied spiritual systems as Vodou and Santería.

The prevalence of Catholic saints and other artifacts in both Vodou and Santería suggests that Catholicism ultimately dominated African beliefs, but the combination is more complex than that. The linguistic situation in Haiti offers a parallel. Haitian Kreyòl was long classified as a Romance language (Hall 11), a pidgin or dialect of French. More recent scholarship on Kreyòl, however, suggests that the lexemes of French have been superimposed onto the structures of West African languages, particularly Ewe and Yoruba, languages of Ghana and Nigeria, respectively (Phillips 39–40). Santería in the Dominican Republic functions in the same way, as a religion in which the Catholic system of saints has been superimposed upon traditional African beliefs in gods and spirits. It is precisely this superimposition that leads to the cultural erasure that syncretism/hybridity suggests; because the nominal system is Christian, the underlying structures and beliefs are hidden and thus dismissed.

Scholarship on Santería and Vodou in the Caribbean reflects the primacy accorded to the paradigm of syncretism, but some scholars have questioned its ideological and historical underpinnings, which have often privileged Europeans, European languages, and Catholicism over the systems already in place or transported geographically from Africa. Miguel Barnet in his study of Santería provides insight into the exchange of culture in both directions. Barnet emphasizes patterns of resistance in the exchange between Africans and the invading Europeans. He argues that Africans, when faced with the dogma of the Catholic Church, "set into motion a most complex sociological phenomenon when they syncretized divinities with the Catholic saints—a give-and-take of elements and attributes that nonetheless did not alter the basic concepts transplanted from Africa" (87). In refusing to alter these basic concepts, Africans resisted the imposition of Catholicism without inspiring the hostility and violence that outright refusal would provoke, and they were thus able to retain their traditions while maintaining the appearance of conversion.

A number of scholars of Caribbean culture and history have pointed out the ideological and political pitfalls that the concept of "syncretic" religions entails. They find the same cultural erasure and uniformity that hybridity suggests insofar as it threatens accurate study, representation, and reality of the region and its cultures. Several scholars have offered alternatives to conceptualizing the spirituality of the various peoples on the islands. George Brandon suggests that "the concept of syncretism hides more than it reveals about Santería while revealing more about Western conceptions of religion and culture than about the cultural reality they are trying to explain" (7). In addition to risking Eurocentrism and the erasure of the African influence, syncretism implies a fusion or an achieved merging of traditions, which Brandon refutes in his work. He has found many practitioners of Santería who "make a distinction between Catholicism and African religions" (168), disproving the completion of the syncretic process and, indeed, of colonial history. I have argued that the experiences of U.S. Caribbean women point to a multiplicity rather than a fusion of identities, and Brandon's study points to a similar phenomenon in Santería as well; he suggests "that syncretism in Santería represents an unresolved conflict, a failed synthesis between African religion and Christianity" (159). Rather than using the concept of syncretism, Brandon prefers to view Santería across "a cultural continuum," in which "the recognition of socially and culturally significant differences in thought and behavior derives from a shared pool of common ideology, history, myth, and contemporary experiences" (7–8). Brandon's continuum thus maintains cultural differences in practice and theory while recognizing what the different peoples might share, particularly in regard to the space of the island. In conceptualizing what the Caribbean shares as well as the variations in Caribbean ideologies, histories, myths, and experiences, Brandon moves toward Franklin Knight's call for the unity of the Caribbean without the concomitant obscuring of racial, national, linguistic, and cultural difference across the region. Alvarez's novels suggest that women who practice Santería see no contradiction and thus no need for integration or suppression of the Catholic tradition and elements of native or African spiritual systems.

Stephen D. Glazier's study of African American religious groups in Trinidad contributes to the notion that religious traditions in contact continue to remain distinct. He, too, has concluded that the term "syncretism" does "not provide the best possible description of what seemed to be occurring at a local level" (50). He recognizes the possibility of the merging of two or more religious traditions, but he points out that "[t]here is also a countervailing tendency for each religious tradition to remain separate" (49–50). In place of syncretism, Glazier draws on Roger Bastide's "'principle of juxtaposition.' In juxtaposition rituals from diverse traditions may be performed within the same religious service, but these rituals must be separated spatially and temporally from one another" (51), further reinforcing distinctions among the traditions.[3] The notion of juxtaposition as Glazier applies it to religious systems creates space for multiple practices that adhere to distinct traditions and identities. Alvarez, however, draws these rituals closer together and contracts the spatial and temporal distances that divide them. She is thus able to maintain the distinctions among the traditions, while demonstrating through accumulation the connections that have survived the loss and displacement that have characterized the region's colonial history.

Glazier's notion of juxtaposition comes out as "symbiosis" in the work of Leslie G. Desmangles.[4] He proposes the application of symbiosis not so much in its biological sense as in its ethnological sense, in which "symbiosis refers to the spatial juxtaposition of diverse religious traditions from two continents, which coexist without fusing into one another" (8). This insistence on the maintenance of distinct traditions reveals an increasing tendency in Caribbean scholarship toward recognizing the histories and cultures that have contributed to the development of a variety of Caribbean religious systems. Patrick Taylor suggests that symbiosis contributes not only to our understanding of religion in the Caribbean but also to our understanding of the Caribbean region in general, arguing in *Nation Dance* that "[t]he idea of symbiosis helps to pull together two apparently opposing schools of Caribbean social and cultural thought: the creolists and the pluralists" (3), who advocate integration and multiplicity, respectively. Symbiosis further suggests interdependence, which grants agency and value to each tradition in contact with one another.

Alvarez has sought to include both the creolists and the pluralists in her construction of mestizaje, a concept that recognizes cultural, racial, and national contact while maintaining these same elements as separate. Mestizaje replaces the "syncretic artifact," which is not synthetic but rather "a signifier made of differences" (Benítez-Rojo 21). Syncretism as Alvarez conceives it thus replaces integration with accumulation. These accumulated differences emerge in Alvarez's work as she explores religion, spirituality, and magic in the lives of Caribbean women both in the islands and in the United States. She includes practices of Vodou, Santería, and Catholicism throughout her fiction, drawing together without fusing or excluding women's agency within these systems.

Joan Dayan's work with Haitian Vodou reveals the connections between religion and politics that have served to create national identity in both the Dominican Republic and Haiti. The political ramifications of constructions of spirituality in Haiti must not be ignored: "In the gritty, not-so-inspiring world of politics and power, a mythologized Haiti of zombies, sorcery, and witchdoctors helps to derail our attention from the real causes of poverty and suffering: economic exploitation, color prejudice, and political guile" (14). On the island of Hispaniola—once called *La Isla Mágica* (Cambeira 211)—magic, religion, and spirituality inform the political, economic, and social constructions of both Haiti and the Dominican Republic.

Ellen McCracken's chapter, "Remapping Religious Space," in *New Latina Narrative* suggests the usefulness of Latina fiction as a means of exploring these systems of spirituality. Part of the project of foregrounding religious differences in their fiction, she argues, serves "to reverse the melting-pot model of integration into U.S. society" (95). Religious motifs "both facilitat[e] narrative memory and serv[e] as totemic signifiers of membership in a group" (McCracken 5); when applied to Alvarez's work, these totemic signifiers point to her understanding of the beliefs that influence Caribbean identity and experience, including Santería, Vodou, and Catholicism. These motifs, however, frequently sustain Latina writers' larger purpose of articulating "a sense of social ethics and a new moral vision sometimes quite different from those of orthodox religion" (McCracken 95). Alvarez contrasts her sense of social ethics to the political terrorism of Trujillo, elaborating through spirituality women's agency in effecting political and social change. Through "magical thinking," the women in her novels engage their religious practices as a means of valuing both women's knowledge and participation in the nation's political and cultural life.

Julia Alvarez is not the first U.S. Latina writer to propose spirituality as a means of "cultural and political resistance," which Theresa Delgadillo has identified in the work of mestiza writer Ana Castillo, specifically in Castillo's novel *So Far From God*. This novel, Delgadillo argues, "challenges pervasive notions of religion as an obstacle to progressive action and perceptions of the sway of Catholicism in Chicana communities. It also asks us to see cultural resistance alongside political resistance, and to recognize women as agents of social change" (888–89). Like Alvarez, Castillo "does not take a syncretic view of spirituality. [. . .] The novel emphasizes differing traditions and practices coexisting in the same world as aspects of the multiple subjectivities that define its characters" (Delgadillo 890).

Alvarez's insistence on the asymptotic nature of the multiple subjectivities of the U.S. Caribbean woman writer corresponds to Castillo's project of valuing the diversity of traditions that shape the Latina identity in the United States. As Castillo values women's spirituality, Alvarez insists on women's autonomy in their own spiritual practices and beliefs. In Alvarez's writings, women control their own spiritual practices, manifest in rituals, prayers, and beliefs that privilege magic, community, and story-telling. Alvarez also seeks to address the intersection between gender and race elaborated in the spiritual practices in Haiti and the Dominican Republic, which allows her through spirituality to explore contestations of history, race, and class in the relationship between the two countries that share the island of Hispaniola.

To write the mestizaje of those religious traditions, Alvarez creates multiple identities, improvisations, histories, genres, and perspectives by consulting powerful signs—stories and memories; she thus engages in "magical thinking." This concept derives from *In the Name of Salomé*, in which Camila Henríquez consults her mother's poems for signs about both the past and the future (31). Thus, magical thinking becomes a way for Alvarez and her characters to privilege literature and memories not just those that Camila seeks in her mother's work but also those that Alvarez examines across postcolonial literature, culture, and identity. Magical thinking becomes a method for constructing the multiple forms of women's spirituality, alternatives to women's subjugation in the dominant religions of the world. Although magic has primarily been viewed in the West as religion's evil opposite, Alvarez brings magic and religion together in her own map of the island. Women's spirituality manifests itself through a variety of practices, beliefs, and knowledge systems that Alvarez gathers together to form the magic of women's lives.

HAITI, THE DOMINICAN REPUBLIC, AND RELIGION DURING THE ERA OF TRUJILLO

The religious practices of the recurring character of Chucha embody in Alvarez's novels the political, economic, and racial interdependence between Dominican and Haitian identity. Narrating a section that takes place in the Dominican Republic in *How the García Girls Lost Their Accents*, the young Fifi notes that "[n]one of the maids liked Chucha because they all thought she was kind of below them, being so black and Haitian and all" (219). Fifi addresses the significant intersection of class, race, and nation that has long influenced identity in the Dominican Republic when she describes Chucha as "super wrinkled and Haitian blue-black, not Dominican *café-con-leche* black" (218). Alvarez describes another maid in the household, Nivea, as "'black-black': my mother always said it twice to darken the color to full, matching strength. She'd been nicknamed Nivea after an American face cream her mother used to rub on her, hoping the milky white applications would lighten her baby's black skin" (260). Nivea's story reflects Alvarez's awareness of the importance of skin color in class hierarchies in the Dominican Republic.

Race and class are inextricable from religion in constructions of Dominican identity and history, both of which are defined against Haiti and Haitians as Other/s. Alvarez explores the political and social construction of race and class in an article she wrote in 1993 for *Essence* magazine, titled "Black Behind the Ears," in which she describes a conversation she witnessed in the Dominican Republic. Two "equally black men" were engaged in an argument that provoked one of the men to hurl a racial epithet at the other. When Alvarez asked her friend, "But aren't they both Black?" her friend replied, "'Oh, no,' he explained. 'The Haitian one is Black, the other one is Dominican'" (129). The construction of Dominican national identity relies on constructions of Haitian identity as black and poor. As David Howard points out in *Coloring the Nation*, *dominicanidad* "represents a celebration of whiteness, Hispanic heritage and Catholicism" (2), a construction that "clashes dramatically with the popular Dominican image of Haiti—one of *negritud* or blackness, vodú and African ancestry" (17). For most Dominicans, blackness cannot be separated from adherence to Vodou, neither of which is extricable from Haitianness. The interconnection among race, religion, and class informs the construction of the nations of Haiti and the

Dominican Republic. The racism that Chucha faces among the other maids the Garcías employ reflects these interconnections, and her religious practices are inextricable from her national and racial identity.

The nationalism that has characterized the Dominican and Haitian experience is largely predicated on memory, recollections of occupation, war, and political struggle. John Augelli suggests that such "[m]emories of bitter conflicts reinforce the national contrasts between Haiti and the Dominican Republic" (21–22). Silvio Torres-Saillant similarly points out that the Dominican national identity is dependent upon Haitians, against whom they define themselves and thereby construct "a nation-building ideology based primarily on self-differentiation from Haiti" (54), in which "anti-Haitianism becomes a form of Dominican patriotism" (55). Trujillo used this anti-African sentiment in his campaign to "whiten" the Dominican Republic;[5] during the trujillato, "anti-Haitianism served a two-fold purpose: to furnish a nationalistic ambience that would stimulate unquestioning patriotism and to provide an international concern around which the Dominican people could be induced to rally so as to quell the forces of potential domestic dissent" (Torres-Saillant 55). The racial division between the two countries emerges in constructions of religion as well. Howard has found that in the Dominican Republic, Vodou "is generally perceived to be a Haitian vice—the black magic of the uncivilized, violent, dangerous African society" (93). This nationalism permeated all levels of society during the trujillato, apparent in Chucha's isolation from the other maids, who would otherwise inhabit her socioeconomic class.

Alvarez describes Chucha's spiritual practices to underscore both her perceived difference from the Dominicans, who not only share an island with Haiti but also a racial and colonial history, and Chucha's refusal to alter her beliefs in order to assimilate into Dominican culture. Fifi observes that "Mami finally had to give her a room to herself because none of the other maids wanted to sleep with her. I can see why they were afraid. The maids said she got mounted by spirits. They said she cast spells on them. And besides, she slept in a coffin" (*García Girls* 219). Fifi's words and the maids' fears reiterate Dayan's contention that pathologizing Vodou and its adherents serves political, economic, and social functions in terms of identifying, oppressing, and exploiting members of certain classes and nations. Although we might view Chucha's exclusion as isolation, another reading of this consequence of Dominican racism, classism, and nationalism suggests Chucha's ability to claim a room of her own. Chucha uses her magic and religion for a variety of projects and retains control over both its power and its purpose. Describing these practices in detail, Alvarez preserves the collective memory of those practices in the narrative space of her novel. The García girls would find in the closet "a jar of something wicked you weren't supposed to touch. Or you'd find a candle burning in her room right in front of someone's picture and a little dish with a cigar on it and red and white crepe streamers on certain days crisscrossing her room" (219). These descriptions also reinforce Chucha's agency, which, despite her social position, she maintains through the power of her rituals. Women may be barred from the institutional practices of the Catholic Church and from many authorized rituals of Vodou, but Chucha protects her right and ability to practice her own beliefs on her own terms.

Alvarez also reveals Chucha as an agent of political change by using Chucha's rituals to undermine the manipulation and control of Trujillo and his henchmen. When Carlos García's participation in a plot to assassinate Trujillo is exposed, Trujillo's military police—the SIM— enter the house and refuse to leave when they do not find Carlos at home. Chucha comes into the room where the SIM are waiting for his return, and "[a]s she exits, she lets drop a fine powder. Her lips move the whole time as if she were doing her usual sullen, under-her-breath grumbling, but Yoyo knows she is casting a spell that will leave the men powerless, becalmed" (*García Girls* 200). Instead of viewing herself as powerless—as she is by the regime that attempted the genocide of her people in 1937—Chucha asserts her own power through Vodou.

To emphasize further Chucha's power as a woman and as a practitioner of Vodou, Alvarez gives Chucha voice at the end of *How the García Girls Lost Their Accents*. Describing the rituals in her own words, Chucha provides the knowledge and perspective of a believer to whom issues of scholarly constructions of syncretism or juxtaposition are irrelevant to its practice. By including Chucha's perspective, Alvarez layers the narrative to disrupt the very notion of "insider" and "outsider," concepts that serve to objectify and render passive those so labeled. As McCracken has pointed out, in *How the García Girls Lost Their Accents*, Alvarez reveals "no privileged readers of those narratives who can be counted on to have 'insider' knowledge of every aspect of religious culture" (95); everyone is an Other. Chucha's voice allows her to describe her own spirituality rather than remaining the silent object of the Garcías' and their maids' scrutiny and distrust; she thus defines for herself who is Other. In her section of the novel, Chucha grieves for the Garcías who have fled: "They have left—and only silence remains, the deep and empty silence in which I can hear the voices of my *santos* settling into the room, of my *loa* telling me stories of what is to come" (222). To ensure peace for the Garcías and for herself, Chucha says "prayers to all the *santos*, to the *loa*, and to the Gran Poder de Dios, visiting each room, swinging the can of cleaning smoke, driving away the bad sprits that filled the house this day" (233). Chucha claims the saints from the jurisdiction of the Catholic Church and appropriates their power for herself and those she loves. She remains faithful still to the *loa* (or *lwa*) that have traveled with her ancestors from Africa to the Caribbean. These words reveal the power of religion at the local level—as local as the individual—by granting the ability to evoke the signification of the practices in her own way, to her own ends, and through her own means. Chucha sees the inhabitants of the United States, where the Garcías will live, as "[t]oo pale to be the living. The color of zombies, a nation of zombies" (221). She effectively uses color to invert the racial stereotype used against Haitians and to claim the power to define her own beliefs and perceptions.

Chucha's ritual beliefs and practices also allow Alvarez to explore Dominican history beyond her own family's experience with the trujillato by including in the narrative the events of the Haitian massacre of 1937.

The Haitian massacre turned on the very issues of race, class, nation, and religion that have long characterized the construction of identity on both sides of Hispaniola. In October of 1937, Trujillo ordered the murder of Haitians living along the Haitian-Dominican border, a campaign that he hoped would contribute to the "whitening" of the nation. Estimates of the number of casualties in the massacre fall between 18,000 and 35,000 (Farmer 103), deaths that Trujillo justified by claiming that "Haitians are foreigners in our land. They are dirty, rustlers of cattle, and practitioners of voodoo. Their presence within the territory of the Dominican Republic cannot but lead to the deterioration of the living conditions of our citizens" (qtd. in Farmer 103). Conflating economic class, race, and religion, Trujillo invoked Vodou as a means of differentiating Dominican and Haitian identity and experience and thereby pathologized the religion for his own political purposes.

Alvarez's allusion to the massacre in *How the García Girls Lost Their Accents* emphasizes Dominican ignorance to the political, racial, and economic tensions at work when Trujillo ordered the Haitians living on the border in the Dominican Republic to be killed. With childlike innocence, Fifi repeats what she has apparently heard others say about Chucha: "She was real Haitian, too, and that's why she couldn't say certain words like the word for parsley" (218). What Fifi omits in her description of Chucha's linguistic abilities is the significance of the word *parsley*; when Trujillo ordered the massacre of the Haitians, the test used by Dominicans demanded that the Haitians pronounce the Spanish word for parsley, *perejil*. Because racial identity in the borderland between the two countries was difficult to determine, Dominicans used this linguistic test—a twentieth-century Shibboleth[6]—to test the cultural, and thus national, identity of those living along the border. Through Chucha's presence in the García household, Alvarez draws Haitian history into her novels of the Dominican Republic written for a North American audience, and she thus expands the community of her narrative beyond the confines of national borders and her own experience. Fifi's knowledge, and perhaps that of most Dominicans for many years during Trujillo's regime, is limited to Chucha's individual experience. Her story begins when "Chucha had just appeared at my grandfather's doorstep one night, asking to be taken in. Turns out it was the night of the massacre when Trujillo decreed that all black Haitians on our side of the island would be executed by dawn. There's a river the bodies were finally thrown into that supposedly runs red to this day" (218). Fifí's knowledge of the Massacre River is only possible twenty-three years after the event, and her understanding remains limited to what she overhears, not what she remembers. The massacre is a gap in Dominican collective memory that Alvarez and other Caribbean writers—notably Haitian writer Edwidge Danticat—have sought to repair.

The allusion to the Haitian massacre fits Alvarez's other purpose in demonstrating Chucha's refusal to assimilate to cultural and, especially, spiritual practices in her adopted country, a resistance that stems from a tradition of rebellion in Haitian history. In constructing their own identity, Haitians look to a long history of rebellion, revolution, and independence. The first country in Latin America to win and declare its independence—the second independent state, after the United States, in the Western Hemisphere—Haiti is a country of people who resisted and continue to resist imperial and patrimonialist domination and interference. The slave rebellion that led to Haiti's independence in 1804 left in its wake many years of instability and political isolation. In order to preserve their independence throughout such volatile times, Haitians progressively dismantled or destroyed the social, political, and economic structures established by the colonial invaders, structures that had created and maintained the plantation system. Haiti, suggests Franklin Knight, was confronted with a hard choice: "independence or general well-being. [. . .] Haitians opted for independence, which meant nothing short of the total physical destruction of every institutional form which made plantation society possible" (63). As a result, there is little evidence that the people of Haiti locate their national identity within physical institutions such as universities, museums, historical markers, or monuments in the same way that Trujillo invested these sites with meaning and history.[7] This sense of rebellion continues to inform Haitian life, engendering a marked disrespect for the very monuments and markers that Trujillo used to foster national identity. In 1986, for example, when a military coup overthrew Haitian President Jean-Claude "Baby Doc" Duvalier, jubilant Haitians "marched to downtown Port-au-Prince and mobbed the statue of Christopher Columbus that the Italian government had helped erect years before. Throngs of exuberant protesters tore the bronze Columbus off his base and cast him into the ocean that had brought him to Hispaniola" (Wucker 76).

Alvarez reveals her commitment to exploring Haitians' role in Dominican collective memory by including the massacre in both *In the Name of Salomé* and *In the Time of the Butterflies*. Camila Henríquez is forced to leave the Dominican Republic at age three, and despite her desire to return as an adult, "Trujillo has made her own country an impossible choice" (*In the Name* 3). She tells a fellow Dominican that she hasn't even been back to visit "'since the massacre,' she explains. The slaughter of Haitians had disturbed her profoundly. What was it Trujillo finally paid for the twenty thousand dead, twenty pesos a head?" (79). These details of the Haitian massacre form a thread across Alvarez's work that reveals her engagement in the multiplicity of identities in the Dominican Republic that is not the white, Spanish nation that Trujillo sought to construct. In the novel, Camila accepts an invitation to speak in 1950 about her mother and to commemorate her mother's poetry, but she spontaneously addresses "the massacre of the Haitians she has never mentioned publicly before" (85). Within Camila's breaking of the silence about the massacre lie Alvarez's own efforts to bring this event in Dominican and Haitian history into the collective memory of Dominicans and North Americans. Understanding these histories and her mother's legacy is precisely the magical thinking that Camila engages in; by consulting her mother's poems, Camila seeks signs of her mother's story, a story that, as Salomé points out at the beginning of her novel, is also the story of the Dominican Republic. Camila's magical thinking rests on her ability to create a history from absence and silence. Alvarez does not portray Camila's religious life in the novel but instead reveals that Camila's faith lies in her relationship to her mother and to her country.

Alvarez links the Haitian massacre to religion in the story of Patria Mirabal's faith in *In the Time of the Butterflies*. Initially believing that she would be called to serve God as a nun, Patria had always been the most faithful of the Mirabal sisters. Even after she decides to be married, Patria sees her faith as her "pearl of great price" (52). Unlike her sister Minerva, Patria is for a long time able to maintain distinctions between her life of faith and the political and social turmoil of Trujillo's regime. She will admit that "El Jefe is no saint, everyone knew that, but among the *bandidos* that had been in the National Palace, this one at least was building churches and schools, paying off our debts" (51). Patria also adheres to the gender ideologies sanctioned by the Church and sees politics, like theology, as a business for men, not women. She tells Minerva, "It's a dirty business, you're right. That's why we women shouldn't get involved" (51). Using both her faith and her gender to justify her social and political apathy, Patria initially maintains the fantasy of peace and prosperity that Trujillo constructs for Dominicans. In time, however, she admits, "Minerva's talk had begun affecting me. I started noting the deadness in Padre Ignacio's voice, the tedium between gospel and communion, the dry papery feel of the host in my mouth. My faith was shifting, and I was afraid" (52). Through Patria's faith, Alvarez alludes to the Catholic Church's initial complicity in Trujillo's regime.

Ultimately, Patria's identity as a woman and a mother becomes the impetus for her understanding of the way her faith had prevented her from seeing the truth of the trujillato. When she miscarries during a pregnancy, Patria associates the loss of the baby with the miscarriage of humanity during Trujillo's regime. She finds herself suddenly crying in Minerva's arms "because I could feel the waters breaking, the pearl of great price slipping out, and I realized I was giving birth to something dead I had been carrying around inside me" (52). The dead thing she had been carrying around was not her faith in God so much as it had been her faith in Trujillo and her belief in his lies. In the same way that

Minerva and María Teresa associate their knowledge of the truth about Trujillo with menstruation and womanhood—the loss of innocence—Patria associates her new understanding of Trujillo with the loss of her baby. Memory is the catalyst for Patria's transformation. As she loses her "pearl of great price," she remembers what she has heard about "thousands of Haitians massacred at the border, making the river, they say, still run red—¡Ay, Dios Santo!" (53). That she invokes God's name proves her continuing faith in her religion but not her country. Of the Haitian massacre, she realizes that "I had heard, but I had not believed. Snug in my heart, fondling my pearl, I had ignored their cries of desolation" (53). Despite the revelation of memory and history that Patria experiences, she is able to reclaim her faith as she looks at the faces of the Dominicans who surround her at Mass as she recognizes the power of community in overcoming the despair of the country. At the church, Patria "turned around and saw the packed pews, hundreds of weary, upturned faces, and it was as if I'd been facing the wrong way all my life" (58). In turning to face the right way, Patria begins a new life of social activism and political commitment, a life driven rather than hindered by her religious faith.

To demonstrate the multiplicity of religious beliefs and practices that characterize the Dominican Republic, Alvarez includes in the novel a local religion that she does not name specifically but that functions alongside Patria's Catholicism. Fela, a black maid in the Mirabal household, provides examples of the practices of that religion. Although her faith differs from Patria's, Fela both understands and influences Patria's faith, particularly when Patria begins to blend her Catholic practices with some rituals that Fela has introduced to the family. As a result of Fela's influence, Patria decides to treat Trujillo "like a spirit worthy of my attention, and maybe he would start behaving himself" (202). Fearful for the members of her family that Trujillo has imprisoned, she sets up an altar below the required portrait of Trujillo, and

> [e]very day I changed the flowers and said a few words. Mama thought I was putting on a show for Peña and his SIM, who

came by often to check on the family. But Fela understood, except she thought I was trying to strike a deal with the evil one. I wasn't at all. I wanted to turn him towards his better nature. (202–3)

Patria again blends her faith with Fela's at a dinner party the Mirabales are forced to throw for one of Trujillo's henchmen. The family is appalled at the idea of entertaining Captain Peña in their home, but Patria has faith that "Fela would sprinkle in her powders and Tono would say an Our Father backwards over the pot, and even I would add some holy water I'd bottled from Jacqueline's baptism" (221). These additions to the Captain's *sancocho* are acts of both magic and rebellion, efforts to control their own *destinos* under a dictator who seeks to deny them control with his every action.

Patria is not the only sister to be influenced by Fela's spiritual practices. Mate requests from her "something I can use to spell a certain bad person." According to Fela's instructions, Mate should "write this person's name on a piece of paper, fold it, and put the paper in my left shoe because that is the foot Eve used to crush the head of the serpent. Then burn it, and scatter those ashes near the hated person" (121). Mate carries out this ritual with a price of paper inscribed with the name *Trujillo*. As had happened with Patria, Mate's spiritual practices—even those borrowed from Fela—are intertwined with the political climate of the time. This practice, with its nominal relationship to Catholicism through the invocation of Eve and the snake, reflects Alvarez's portrait of the Dominican people's resistance to both Trujillo's regime and colonial domination. Mate's practice would not have been sanctioned by the Catholic Church hierarchy, and these rituals thus undermine Church hierarchies of gender that exclude women in the practice of their own faith.

After the assassination of the Mirabal sisters, Fela uses her blend of magic and spirituality to blur the distinctions between the worlds of the living and the dead and to draw on the power the girls represented during their lives, a power that only increases after their deaths. Fela sets up "an altar with pictures of the girls cut out from the popular posters that appeared each November. Before them, a table was laid out, candles and the mandatory cigar and bottle of rum. But most frightening was the picture of Trujillo that had once hung on Dedé and Jaimito's wall" (64). This altar reveals the role of culture—in this case popular culture—in the practice of religion, as Fela uses photos of the girls taken from public posters. The presence of Trujillo's portrait points to both Fela's and Alvarez's insistence on the artificiality of barriers between religion and politics. Fela moves beyond the altar to spirit possession, which alarms Dedé, who thinks, "Possessed by the spirits of the girls, can you imagine! People were coming from as far away as Barahona to talk 'through' this ebony black sibyl with the Mirabal sisters" (63). Spirit possession is a particular hallmark of Vodou as practiced in Haiti, and Dedé's remark about Fela's skin color as well as her position as maid in the Mirabal household suggests Fela's Haitian origin. Although almost certainly marginalized by Dominican society, Fela would have enjoyed a certain authority among believers because of her nationality and culture. Through Fela's work with the dead, "[c]ures had begun to be attributed to Patria; María Teresa was great for love woes; as for Minerva, she was competing with the Virgencita as Patroness of Impossible Causes" (63). These cures draw from the experiences of the sisters' lives, and their powers after death increase both in the realm of the spiritual and the political.

Most important in the novel, perhaps, is Fela's role in preserving the memory of the sisters. Dedé is certainly the guardian of their memory, but Fela's magic keeps them alive for the people of the Dominican Republic who cannot visit the museum or attend state functions to honor the political work of the Mirabal sisters, which in turn dismantles the rigid class distinctions in the country. Minerva's daughter, Minou, speaks to her mother and aunts through Fela, maintaining a connection to the women she lost as a young child and creating a memory that does not otherwise exist for her. On one visit to Dedé, Minou is upset because the spirits "wouldn't come. Fela says they must finally be at rest. It was strange hearing that. I felt sad instead of glad" (174).

When Minou loses her mother's spiritual visits, she also loses the memory of her mother. For her, the memory is kept alive through the merging of her own faith with Fela's religious practices.

Magical Thinking: Spirituality and Storytelling

Alvarez ultimately reveals memory to be a kind of magic, related to Fela's spirituality. As the surviving sister, Dedé comes to see herself as a kind of medium, a magical connection to the memory of her sisters. After the girls are assassinated, people from all over the country arrive to tell Dedé their stories, which I have argued allows her to create her own memory of their last afternoon. One such visitor, Mateo Nuñez,

> had just begun listening to the Sacred Rosary on his little radio when he heard the terrible crash. He learned about the trial of the murderers on the same radio. He walked from his remote mountain shack with his shoes in a paper sack so as not to wear them out. It must have taken him days. He got a lift or two, here and there, sometimes going the wrong way. He hadn't traveled much off the mountain. I saw him out the window when he stopped and put on his shoes to show up proper at my door. He gave me the exact hour and made the thundering noise of the tumbling Jeep he graphed with his arching hand. Then he turned around and headed back to his mountain.
>
> He came all that way just to tell me that. (303)

Many such stories follow. Eventually, however, Dedé turns from the listener to the speaker, transformed into "the oracle" (312). Dedé comes to understand the cause of this transformation and comes to identify Dominicans as "a broken people," in need of the kind of magic that storytelling can bring. She tells a friend, "We had lost our hope, and we needed a story to understand what had happened to us" (313); Alvarez thus reinforces the assertion she makes about fiction as a way of understanding the trujillato. Dedé understands that the magic of the memory of sisters persists despite their silence at Fela's altar. At night, she believes, "I hear them just as I'm falling asleep. Sometimes, I lie at the very brink of forgetfulness, waiting, as if their arrival is my signal that I can fall asleep" (321). She recognizes "[t]heir different treads, as if even spirits retained their personalities, Patria's sure and measured step, Minerva's quicksilver impatience, Mate's playful little skip" (321). Remembering, for Dedé, is magical thinking.

The magical thinking that Alvarez describes in the Dominican Republic follows her characters into exile in the United States. Another maid in the employ of the Garcías, Primi, appears in both *¡Yo!* and *How the García Girls Lost Their Accents*. Primi's daughter, Sarita, speculates in *¡Yo!* about the role magic plays in her mother's voyage from the Dominican Republic to the United States with the García family. When various members of the family would make trips to New York City before their exile, Primi would pack the suitcases and

> sprinkle in a special powder made of her ground fingernails and bits of her hair and some other elements the santera had charged her twenty pesos to prepare. It worked. Over the years, all those little bits and pieces of my mother collected in New York and set up a force of attraction that finally drew the rest of her to the magic city. (54)

Primi remains separate from the Garcías by class, indicated both by the name and by her status in the household. Unlike Chucha, however, Primi practices Santería, which would place her, in terms of class hierarchy, above Chucha and other Haitians who practice Vodou, although Alvarez does not privilege either of these two religions.

Both Primi and Chucha have influenced the García girls, particularly Yolanda, in their own brand of magical thinking. As a young girl, Yo frequently sneaks into her father's study to look at his medical books. He notices "her lips moving, an endless mumble going on as she turned the pages" (*¡Yo!* 300). When he asks her what she is whispering, Yo replies,

"I'm telling the sick people stories to make them feel better." This response thrills her father, who says, "My face lit up with pleasure at knowing that one of my children had inherited that sense of magic" (300). The sense of magic that Carlos sees is Yolanda's imagination, but this scene from Yo's early life also suggests Alvarez's insistence on the connection between storytelling and healing.

As a struggling writer, Yolanda performs her own healing rituals, circling a house with a girlfriend to protect the space of the new apartment where she is living. The magic extends beyond Yolanda's protection when her landlady's errant husband, Clair, returns to her. Because Yolanda does not have a voice in ¡Yo!, the story comes from her landlady, who says, "Now, I don't go in for hocus pocus one bit, but next thing I know, I hear the pickup up front, and there's Clair minus the girlfriend" (158). Not only has Clair returned, but the landlady has also found her own voice, breaking the silence that has for years obscured his infidelity and cruelty. She doesn't "know if it's the magic powders or just having those girls around two weeks now, but I find I have a mouth" (158). What gives her voice, Alvarez suggests, may be the community of women. The real magic lies in the power of women's support and spirituality.

Yolanda herself, in blessing another house where she lives with her husband, is looking for magic, inspiration, and power for her poetry. Around the yard, she buries "power bundles, the remains of spells, mal ojos that need to be dispersed" (¡Yo! 259). Her husband, who observes these rituals, understands that Yolanda "is not a wannabe witch and she is not a leftover hippy," but "[t]hese superstitions—he must call them that—are part of her island background" (259–60). As a North American, her husband uses the word "superstition" to indicate that these practices are above—or beyond—belief, with the denotation of irrationality. But Yolanda, who would certainly identify with her Catholic upbringing, has indeed been influenced by her "island background," a culture that often does not distinguish the magic of prayer from the magic of spells or the power of powders and potions from the power of holy water and anointing oil.

Yolanda's father also engages in magical thinking to influence her writing life. His "magical solution" is to give her his blessing, which will "make the curse of doubt go away" (296). Carlos García fears that his efforts to silence Yolanda in the Dominican Republic will silence her writer's voice as well, and he hopes that this blessing will cure the effects of that silence. As she has with Fela's magic, with the Mirabal sisters' beliefs, and with Yolanda's spirituality, Alvarez draws together different beliefs into Carlos's magical thinking—the blessing, derived from the Catholic Church, and the terms "magical" and "curse" that draw from the "island background" that he and his daughter share. Both Yolanda and her father link these magical solutions to Yolanda's art and thus reveal the connection that Alvarez makes between magic and storytelling in her own writings.

Alvarez explores the explicit connection between magic and storytelling in her children's book *How Tía Lola Came to Visit Stay*. When Miguel's Tía Lola comes from the Dominican Republic to visit the Guzmán family for a while, he is embarrassed by how different she is from the North Americans who surround him in Vermont. When she arrives, she cleanses the basement, to "cast out any bad spirit and attract good spirits and magical *ciguapas* from the island" (20). She brings with her "several jars with odd ingredients, which Mami says are probably potions. Tucked in the bottom [of her suitcase] is a bottle of *Agua de Florida*, which Tía Lola sprinkles around the room" (15). Miguel looks askance at his mother, who responds, "'It's good-luck water,' Mami explains. Tía Lola is something of a *santera*. 'It's like a doctor who works with magic instead of medicine'" (15). Miguel is not particularly interested in Santería or the mestizaje of religious traditions and practices in the country that he sometimes calls home. He is, however, interested in his aunt's stories—the uncle with six fingers, "the cousin who once befriended a *ciguapa* with pastelitos" (18). Despite the potions and spells Tía Lola brings with her, Miguel finds that "[w]hat is most magical is how, even though in his daily conversations with Tía Lola, Miguel sometimes doesn't understand Tía Lola's Spanish, still when she tells stories, Miguel seems to understand every word" (18). Similarly, she and her new English-speaking friend Becky "aren't speaking the same language and yet they seem to understand each other perfectly!" (45). Eventually, Miguel concludes that "[h]is aunt is working magic on everybody" (49) through her storytelling. Tía Lola eventually confides her secret in Miguel, a secret that ties together her Santería and the teachings of the Catholic Church, brings together the multiple languages and cultures of the Caribbean and the United States, and emphasizes the multiplicity of magical traditions in both cultures and countries—"Todo es mágico si se hace con amor" (53). [Everything is magic if it is done with love.] Tía Lola's magical thinking connects magic and storytelling to family and love.

Alvarez's magical thinking permits her to question distinctions between magic and reality, particularly in regard to such practices as sanctioning an official Truth for history or religion, insisting on the cultural erasure that "synthesis" suggests, and maintaining class and race hierarchies that serve to separate, rather than unify, the diverse peoples of the Caribbean and the United States. She even draws magic into her project of writing a new place on the map. Alvarez begins *How the García Girls Lost Their Accents* with Yolanda's return trip to the Dominican Republic in search of her cultural and national identity as well as the memories she is missing of her island home. At a party to celebrate her arrival, Yolanda's family presents her with a cake in the shape of the island. She finds that "[b]efore her blazes the route she has worked out on the map for herself" (11), the trip she wants to take across the island. As her family brings out the cake with five candles burning—for the five years since her last visit or for the five major cities of the Dominican Republic—Yolanda takes a deep breath and uses her own magical thinking: "Let this turn out to be my home, Yolanda wishes" (11). Bringing together the cake map—a domestic version linked to the family and the home—and magic, Alvarez reminds us that mapping is a kind of magical thinking in its suggestion that the multiplicity of races, classes, nationalities, cultures, religions, and ideologies can be contained within the lines of a map and the name of a country.

She draws these same issues together in *How Tía Lola Came to ~~Visit~~ Stay* when Tía Lola sows a garden in the shape of Hispaniola. In Tía Lola's magical thinking, "[f]or the border between the Dominican Republic and its neighbor, Haiti, she orders a special kind of rosebush without thorns. 'For a rosier future between the two countries,' she explains in Spanish. She reserves her hot chili peppers for the spot where the capital would be. 'Para los politicos por las mentiras que dicen'" [For the lies the politicians tell] (67). Tía Lola is mapping a new country of her own, one in which the magic of flowers and food can solve political, racial, and national conflicts. Tía Lola's project reflects Alvarez's own efforts to write a new place on the map. While Tía Lola maps the country with vegetables and flowers, Alvarez maps a new space through narrative, creating in her writings not only a geographical but also a social, religious, woman-centered, artistic, racial, political, historical map of the Dominican Republic and the United States.

The spirituality that Alvarez maps throughout these novels points to Alvarez's remembered past—the diversity of practices in her homeland of the Dominican Republic. Attesting to the mestizaje—but not the hybridity—of women's spirituality, these practices followed her to the United States and have permeated her fiction. Chucha and Fela's Vodou practices, side by side with Patria's Catholicism and Tía Lola's Santería, present a convergence of women's experiences, particularly those traditionally marginalized by socioeconomic, racial, and national identity. Alvarez locates that convergence within the narrative space of her novels, a space that entextualizes the experiences, gives multiple women voices, and validates all spiritual practices as demonstrations of subjectivity and independence in the face of colonial oppression. Moreover, Alvarez engages in preservation work by illuminating these practices as part of the collective memory that threatens to disappear—into hybridity—in the face of official History and master narratives. ⌒

Conclusion

Improvising New Maps

Through her diverse and rich body of writings, Julia Alvarez has placed herself at the forefront of a movement to expand the cartographic and conceptual borders of American literature. The multiplicity of Alvarez's work resonates with the work of many contemporary U.S. writers who inscribe in their works an increasingly fragmented postmodern world. Alvarez's vision, however, redeems the contradictions of postmodern identity by suggesting their potential for creativity, collective memory, spirituality, and especially literature. The tensions developed through her narratives—between individual and community, nation and place, history and literature, tradition and innovation—also emerge in the work of a diverse group of contemporary writers, revealing her crucial place in an expanding literary cartography of the Americas. Alvarez's work thus suggests the necessity of broadening U.S. literary history to accommodate that evolving cartography. Her connections to writers across cultural and national boundaries reveal her desire not to replace traditional writers in classrooms and anthologies but to join them, adding her voice to a long literary tradition.[1]

Alvarez addresses issues of concern not only to contemporary U.S. authors but also to Latin America, Caribbean, and Latino/a writers, joining these various literary traditions. American literary history—in the largest sense of the term *American*—has been marked by two "booms," first for Latin American writers in the 1960s, and then for Latino/a writers in the 1990s. Out of these two booms, a significant corpus of criticism and theory has emerged about postcolonial nations and their struggles for independence and self-definition. It is within this context that the term *hybridity* has been applied and then contested, suggesting that its usefulness may have waned over time. In place of hybridity, Alvarez provides a kind of asymptotic mestizaje as a theoretical paradigm for understanding her work. While her writings do not appear immediately tied to the Latin American writers of the 1960s, whose work is often characterized by its use of magical realism, her concern with dictatorship and nation reveal strong ties to the postcolonial history of countries previously colonized by Spain.

Alvarez also claims membership in the growing community of Latina authors writing in the United States, who share her focus on language, women's creativity, and cultural preservation. For Alvarez, the *bruja* of Judith Ortiz Cofer's *In the Line of the Sun*, a novel that Alvarez greatly admires, shares literary space with the spiritual practices of Alvarez's characters. Sandra Cisneros's *Caramelo* relies on memory and material history and thus seeks to join Alvarez's *In the Time of the Butterflies* in augmenting and contradicting traditional discourses of history in the postcolonial Americas. Ana Castillo in *So Far From God* writes a linguistic mestizaje of Chicano Spanish and English in her lexical and syntactic choices, a style that resonates with and against Alvarez's Caribbean varieties. These authors, among others, form for Alvarez a "*comunidad* in the word" (*Something* 169) that she sees as integral to her own identity as a writer. By defining her identity as communal, Alvarez recognizes the value of interaction and conversation among and across multiple discourse communities as part of the project of creating literature. Authorship, she suggests, ultimately may not be merely an individual endeavor.

There are many other writers outside this Latina comunidad to whom Alvarez feels connected, among them Walt Whitman, Emily Dickinson, Michael Ondaatje, Maxine Hong Kingston, Edwidge Danticat, Billy Collins, Seamus Heaney, James Joyce, Marcel Proust, Robert Frost, José Martí, Clarice Lispector, Gabriel García Marquez, Wei T'ai, George Orwell, Mark Twain, D. H. Lawrence, Samuel Johnson, J. D. Salinger, Salman Rushdie, Toni Morrison, and Elizabeth Bishop.[2] Such a list demonstrates Alvarez's commitment to a community of world writers whose work she speaks to in her own writings while maintaining her membership among a group that has called itself "las girlfriends."[3] Across space, time, and culture, Alvarez suggests the balance that must be struck between "identity politics" and an increasingly global society in which literature must be accessible, meaningful, and multiple.

The new place on the map that Julia Alvarez creates where these identities meet is actually a composite or an accumulation of maps that she brings together into the narrative space of her work. Susan Nanamore Maher in "Deep Mapping the Great Plains" asserts that "[a]ny map is a composite map" (17)—a culmination of experience and narratives and memories—and Alvarez writes just such a map against the tradition of colonial mapping and exploration that has excluded so many peoples and cultures. Alvarez herself is writing a map in the tradition of deep maps, which, in Maher's words, "capture within their narrative structures a complex web of information, interpretation, and storytelling. Their cross-sections articulate scientific perspectives, national as well as personal history and mythology, dream time and vision, as well as layers of time both humanly brief and geologically deep" (7). Just as Anzaldúa conceives the relationship between community and mestizaje, Alvarez has mapped, and thus claimed, her own communities across the Americas. Alvarez makes her new map inclusive, drawing together without fusing the many peoples and cultures of the Americas that have traditionally been excluded from historical, literary, and religious discourses since colonization.

Throughout her writings, Alvarez expands traditional constructions of the Caribbean, both in the islands and in the United States. She also simultaneously enlarges the term mestizaje to emphasize the positive power of the multiplicities of cultures, nations, races, religions, arts, languages, and memories of postcolonial peoples. In transforming what Gómez-Vega calls the "wreckage of history"[4]—from colonization to the forced economic and political migrations of the twentieth century—into new stories, Alvarez recasts that wreckage into art. While the colonizers' maps proclaimed permanent occupation, Alvarez writes a map in flux that in its very flexibility accommodates the accumulation of the

Caribbean and multiple destinies, possibilities, and alternatives for U.S. Caribbean women writers.

Alvarez's commitment to write a new place on the map is also revealed in her collection of poetry, published in 2004, *The Woman I Kept to Myself*. Across these seventy-five poems, she returns to the themes of her earlier writings—exile, creativity, language, memory, and storytelling—and further expands her narrative space by working with this material on the page. As she writes in the title poem of the volume, when her mother told her as a child, "Keep it to yourself," Alvarez "turned to this paper solitude/ where I both keep things secret and broadcast/ my love for all the world to read. And so/ through many drafts, I became the woman/ I kept to myself" (36). The tension between silence and language, the Real World and the word, are negotiated in those drafts, which are not obliterated by her final draft but gradually revealed and built upon across the whole of her work. In her return to these same narrative spaces, she seeks redemption, the topic of the final poem in the collection, "Did I Redeem Myself?" She addresses the first two stanzas to her parents and sisters. The final one, however, maps that redemption across the spaces and places of her life:

> But harder still, my two Americas.
> Quisqueya, did I pay my debt to you,
> drained by dictatorship and poverty
> of so much talent? Did I get their ear
> telling your stories to the sultan's court
> until they wept our tears? And you, Oh Beautiful,
> whose tongue wooed me to service, have I proved
> my passion would persist beyond my youth?
> Finally, my readers, what will you decide
> when all that's left of me will be these lines? (156)

These lines map Alvarez's countries, her communities, her histories, her languages, and her writings as she weaves together the stories of her two homelands. Significantly, redemption for Alvarez lies in her own narrative acts—she redeems herself through storytelling rather than waiting for it to be bestowed upon her through assimilation in the United States or return to the Dominican Republic; Alvarez abandons neither and seeks to redeem not only herself but her two Americas.

Alvarez's mappings thus demonstrate the need to appreciate the linkages between theory and practice. In insisting on theoretical as well as narrative agency, she joins many Latina and African American feminists who have argued that the division between theory and art is artificial and counterproductive. Creating both theory and narrative, Alvarez maps an asymptosy of her own through which to understand place, exile, identity, language, memory, genre, and spirituality. When writers create a theoretical model within their writings, they claim greater voice and control over the deployment of their own work. Alvarez's work with space reminds us of the consequences of contests for space and independence, consequences that exceed literary studies and reveal the politics of space in global, and multiple, migrations. Asymptosy, she demonstrates, illustrates the nature not only of exile but also of relations between polities in a post-exploration, post-Conquest, postcolonial world. What divides us becomes increasingly small, perhaps, but significant distances remain within rampant and terrifying political, economic, and social disparities. While her work demonstrates the importance of mestizaje as a means of community-building, she also makes clear the disjunctions that continue to divide many of the earth's people.

Alvarez's improvisations interpret culture for these various communities. Rather than "translating" her Caribbean experience into English, she improvises the various places, histories, genres, and cultures into narrative. Similarly, in her novel *The House on the Lagoon*, Puerto Rican writer Rosario Ferré creates a would-be historian who insists that "literature never changes anything, but history can alter the course of events" (311). As Alvarez demonstrates in her own work, literature can indeed change the course of events and alter the perspective through which we view them. By improvising discourses of the personal and national history of the Americas, Alvarez develops a postcolonial consciousness that is simultaneously independent of and contingent upon geography. The paradox of Alvarez's narrative space lies in the fact that her work is historically and geographically grounded at the same time that it is imaginative and innovative; she is creating constantly novel traditions of postcolonial writing in the Americas. Charting her journey through genre, memory, language, borderlands, and exile, Alvarez has indeed created for herself, and for all of us, a "new place on the map." ⌒

Notes

Introduction

1. On her web site, Alvarez writes that the biography on the flap of *How the García Girls Lost Their Accents* "mentioned that I was raised in the D.R., and a lot of bios after that changed raised to born, and soon I was getting calls from my mother."

2. The farm, Alta Gracia, had been for sale briefly in 2003, but its web site now claims that the farm is "thriving despite the lowest coffee prices in 40 years." Still, as of April 2004, Alvarez and Eichner announced that they "are ready to sell a few prime parcels" so that others can be involved in their efforts toward sustainability, conservation, and fair trade.

3. The farm's web site explains that the Foundation Alta Gracia is supported by coffee sales, funding both a library and a school for local children and adults and for foreign students to learn about sustainability. In January 2000, for example, Alvarez led a group of Middlebury students for a "Writing in the Wilds" workshop where they both wrote and worked on the farm (Jones 1).

4. Deixis is a linguistic term for the changing and relative position of the referents of certain pronouns and locations. The meaning of I, you, we, and they vary according to context, as do the objective pronouns—me, her, him, and them. Other deictic pronouns include this, that, here, and there, each of which is defined according to the speaker or writer's position relative to audience. The unstable and shifting meanings of these referents of these words emphasizes the significance of place and relationships in the context of narrative.

5. DeLoughrey cites Brathwaite's description from an interview in which Brathwaite describes the concept of tidalectics as "the movement of the water backwards and forwards as a kind of cyclic . . . motion, rather than linear" (qtd. in DeLoughrey 18). See Braithwaite in "Interview."

6. Although it is impossible to write theory completely "from within," that is, entirely without influence from the dominant culture, Anzaldúa and other Latino/a writers have insisted on efforts at doing so—from within their culture, their narratives, and their communities.

7. Literary criticism on the concept of deterritorialization has emerged out of readings of Gilles Deleuze and Félix Guattari in *A Thousand Plateaus: Capitalism and Schizophrenia*.

8. Bakhtin defines dialogism as "the characteristic epistemological mode of a world dominated by heteroglossia. Everything means, is understood, as part of a

greater whole—there is a constant interaction between meanings, all of which have the potential of conditioning others" (*Dialogic* 426).

CHAPTER ONE

1. See J. Michael Dash's excellent Introduction to his book *The Other America: Caribbean Literature in a New World Context* for an extended evaluation of the concepts of New World and Old World for literature, history, and culture.

2. See Deleuze and Guattari and Nestor Garcia Canclini's *Hybrid Cultures: Strategies for Entering and Leaving Modernity*. Canclini "bring[s] together such heterogeneous spaces" as cities, museums, schools, and theaters to reorder "the public and the private in the urban space" and to deterritorialize "symbolic processes" (10).

3. See Jacqueline Stefanko and Fernando Valerio Holguín for their assertions of hybridity in Alvarez's work.

4. Significant work has also been done on Sandra Cisneros's *The House on Mango Street* and Ana Castillo's *So Far From God*, scholarship that draws on bell hooks's concept of the home as a site of resistance. In addition to hooks, see Carmela Delia Lanza's essay on *So Far From God*, my essay on Ana Castillo's work in general, and Julian Olivares's and Jacqueline Doyle's essays on Cisneros.

CHAPTER TWO

1. In her 2004 collection of poetry, *The Woman I Kept to Myself*, Alvarez also begins with an epigraph from Milosz: "To whom do we tell what happened on earth?" This collection was released in April 2004, just as this manuscript was going to press.

2. Alvarez notes in her autobiographical information on her web site that her parents returned to the Dominican Republic when she was just three months old because they "prefer[ed] the dictatorship of Trujillo to the U.S.A. of the early 50s."

3. The relationship between the United States and Trujillo's regime as it appears in Alvarez's work is explored in some detail in Chapter 4. For excellent and detailed historical accounts of that relationship, see also Stephen G. Rabe, Raymond H. Pulley, and Eric Roorda.

4. See Linda Kerber and Lynn Hunt.

5. Holloway and Kneale quote from Bakhtin's *Problems of Dostoevsky's Poetics*, in which Bakhtin suggests Dostoevsky's works "have novelness in abundance," as Holloway and Kneale put it (77) because the voices of Dostoevsky demonstrates "[a] plurality of independent and unmerged voices and consciousness," each "with equal rights and each with its own world" (Bakhtin, Problems 6).

6. Barbara Welter and Caroll Smith-Rosenberg began in the 1966 and 1975, respectively, the ground-breaking work on separate spheres that would generate research and scholarship on the topic for the next forty years; see also Jeanne Boydston.

7. See Sandra M. Gilbert and Susan Gubar.

8. Heilbrun credits the work of Tom Driver in *Liberating Rites: Understanding the Transformative Power of Ritual.*

CHAPTER THREE

1. See Edward Said's "Traveling Theory" in *The World, the Text, and the Critic.*

2. The tension between the labels of exile, immigrant, and refugee has a significant impact on the lives of those arriving in the United States from their homelands in the Americas. Until the 1990s, Cubans have been welcomed in the United States as exiles, while Salvadorans have traditionally been labeled economic refugees rather than political exiles and denied legal entry into the United States even during the civil war that displaced five hundred thousand Salvadorans.

3. In "Passing On," a poem in *The Woman I Kept to Myself,* Alvarez refers to her own mother's "malapropping her clichés" (139).

CHAPTER FOUR

1. For a fictionalized account of the massacre, see Haitian writer Edwidge Danticat's excellent novel, *The Farming of Bones.*

2. In contextualizing Alvarez's work within the larger tradition of Latina writing, Elizabeth Coonrod Martínez recognizes that "[g]overnments and histories forget women, but Latina writers are repairing that amnesia" (270). This list suggests that a variety of Caribbean women writers have undertaken the same task.

3. This nickname refers to a story about how Trujillo, as a child, collected *chapitas,* slang for bottlecaps, which he purportedly wore on his chest as medals. As a dictator, he repeatedly revealed the same predilection for flaunting a chest full of honorary and military decorations.

4. In Catholic doctrine, the Immaculate Conception actually refers to Mary's having been conceived without the stain of original sin. Minerva's doctrinal mistake points perhaps to her own innocence about sexual reproduction—or the absence of such innocence.

5. November 25, the day the Mirabal sisters were murdered, has been designated by the United Nations as International Day for the Elimination of Violence against Women. The day thus serves to commemorate simultaneously the Mirabales and all women who have been victims of violence.

6. United States Secretary of State Cordell Hull, as Alvarez notes, once said "Trujillo is an SOB, but he's our SOB" (*Something* 108), a statement often attributed to Franklin Delano Roosevelt.

7. Many Spanish-speakers can also read the novel in a widely available Spanish paperback edition.

Chapter Five

1. When she was honored with the Sor Juana Award in 2002, she said that before writing *In the Time of the Butterflies*, she first wrote a poem for each sister out of which emerged the longer narrative in the novel.

2. The Latina writers particularly associated with generic transgressions are Chicana and mestiza writers who include a variety of genres within a single work to resist the constraints of traditional constructions of race, culture, nation, gender, and sexuality—such as Gloria Anzaldúa's *Borderlands/La Frontera* and Cherrié Moraga's *Loving in the War Years*. While critics have widely discussed the way Anzaldúa and Moraga draw on various genres in their work, they have so far virtually ignored Alvarez's poetry, children's books, and personal and professional essays.

3. The "Housekeeping" poems appear in *Homecoming: New and Collected Poems*.

4. Alvarez continues to rework familiar material in *The Woman I Kept to Myself*: several poems deal with her experiences with English and Spanish; one poem is titled "First Muse," which is the title of one of her essays in *Something to Declare*; in "Museo del Hombre" she addresses the connection between family and national history as it appears in the national museum in Santo Domingo and mentions Salomé Ureña; and in "Passing On," she returns to both her mother's difficulty with clichés and the women in her family's penchant for cooking and creating.

5. Other Caribbean books written especially for young adult readers include Haitian writer Edwidge Danticat's *Behind the Mountains*, Cuban American Ana Veciana-Suárez's *Flight to Freedom*, and Puerto Rican writer Judith Ortiz Cofer's *Call Me María*, all of which appear in the First Person Fiction series. It is important to remember, however, that many bookstores and libraries categorize works by U.S. Latina writers as fiction for adolescents or young adults, including such books as Sandra Cisneros's *The House on Mango Street* and Esmeralda Santiago's *When I Was Puerto Rican*, as well as Alvarez's *How the García Girls Lost Their Accents*.

6. Alvarez has also called this book a "green fable," further expanding its accumulation of genres (Alvarez and Eichner np).

Chapter Six

1. See *The Location of Culture* (5).

2. Alternate spellings of *vodou* include the Americanized *voodoo* and *vodoun*, the latter of which is an attempt to make the Haitian word conform to the French phonological system. Throughout this study, I use Caribbean scholar Joan Dayan's spelling of the word, which she explains in her excellent book *Haiti, History and the Gods*.

3. See Bastide's *The African Religions in Brazil: Toward a Sociology of the Interpretation of Civilizations*.

4. Desmangles also draws on the work of Bastide.

5. Trujillo hid his own Haitian heritage by wearing pancake makeup to lighten his complexion.

6. Judges 12:1–15.

7. See my essay "Both Sides of the Massacre: Collective Memory and Narrative on Hispaniola."

Conclusion

1. Alvarez considers that literary tradition in "Canons," a poem that appears in *The Woman I Kept to Myself*. She writes, "Especially when I peruse/ my old Norton anthologies and note/ the shameful absence of certain voices,/ I wonder if they never existed/ or if they were knocked out of the running/ for some silliness like the writer's sex?" (64).

2. Alvarez refers to all of these authors at least once in her work and to some of them in multiple works.

3. See Melita Marie Garza (5:1).

4. Gómez-Vega borrows this concept from Walter Benjamin.

WORKS CITED

Abbeville, Nicolas Sanson d'. *Amerique, en Plusieurs Cartes Nouvelles*. Paris: Sanson, 1656.

Almánzar, José Alcántara. "Los Escritores Dominicanos bajo la Dictadura de Trujillo." *Revista/Review Interamericana* 21.1–2 (1991): 97–109.

Alvarez, Julia. Address. Sor Juana Award. Mexican Fine Arts Center Museum, Chicago. 9 Oct. 2002.

———. *Before We Were Free*. New York: Knopf, 2002.

———. "Black Behind the Ears." *Essence* (February 1993): 42.

———. *A Cafecito Story*. White River Junction, VT: Chelsea Green, 2001.

———. *En el Tiempo de las Mariposas*. Trans. Rolando Costa Picazo. New York: Plume, 1998.

———. *Homecoming: New and Collected Poems*. New York: Plume, 1996. [1984]

———. "How I Learned to Cook." *The New Family Cookbook*. Ed. Bill Eichner. White River Junction, VT: Chelsea Green, 2000. vx–xix.

———. *How the García Girls Lost Their Accents*. New York: Plume, 1991.

———. *How Tía Lola Came to ~~Visit~~ Stay*. New York: Knopf, 2001.

———. "Julia Alvarez." Available at <http://www.alvarezjulia.com> 22 March 2004.

———. *In the Name of Salomé*. Chapel Hill: Algonquin Books of Chapel Hill, 2000.

———. *In the Time of the Butterflies*. New York: Plume, 1994.

———. *The Other Side/El Otro Lado*. New York: Plume, 1995.

———. "Silver Linings." *New Mexico Humanities Review* (Winter 1994): 77–80.

———. *Something to Declare*. Chapel Hill: Algonquin Books of Chapel Hill, 1998.

———. "Ten of My Writing Commandments." *English Journal* (November 1998): 36–41.

———. *The Woman I Kept to Myself*. Chapel Hill: Algonquin Books of Chapel Hill, 2004.

———. *¡Yo!* New York: Plume, 1997.

Alvarez, Julia, and Bill Eichner. "Café Alta Gracia." Available at <http://www.cafealtagracia.com> 25 March 2004.

Álvarez-Borland, Isabel. "Displacements and Autobiography in Cuban-American Fiction." *World Literature Today* (Winter 1994): 45–49.

Anville, Jean Baptiste Bourguignon d'. *[Atlas.]* Paris: ca. 1776.

Anzaldúa, Gloria. *Borderlands/La Frontera: The New Mestiza*, 2nd ed. San Francisco: Aunt Lute Books, 1999.

Augelli, John P. "Nationalization of Dominican Borderlands." *Geographica Review* 70.1 (1980): 19–35.

Bakhtin, Mikhail. *The Dialogic Imagination.* Trans. Caryl Emerson and Michael Holquist. Austin: U of Texas P, 1981.

———. *Problems of Dostoevsky's Poetics.* Ed. and Trans. Caryl Emerson. Minneapolis: U of Minnesota P, 1984.

Barak, Julia. "'Turning and Turning in the Widening Gyre': A Second Coming into Language in Julia Álvarez's *How the García Girls Lost Their Accents.*" *MELUS* 23.1 (Spring 1998): 159–76.

Barnet, Miguel. "La Regla de Ocha: The Religious System of Santería." *Sacred Possessions: Vodou, Santería, and the Caribbean.* Ed. Margarite Fernandez Olmos and Lizabeth Paravisini-Gebert. New Brunswick, NJ: Rutgers UP, 1997. 79–100.

Bastide, Roger. *The African Religions in Brazil: Toward a Sociology of the Interpretation of Civilizations.* Baltimore: Johns Hopkins UP, 1978.

Behar, Ruth. "Revolutions of the Heart." *The Women's Review of Books* 12.8 (May 1995): 6–7.

Benjamin, Walter. "Theses on the Philosophy of History." *Illuminations.* Trans. Harry Zohn. New York: Harcourt Brace Javanovich, 1968. 253–64.

Benítez-Rojo, Antonio. *The Repeating Island: The Caribbean and the Postmodern Perspective,* 2nd ed. Durham: Duke UP, 1996.

Bernard-Donals, Michael, and Richard Glejzer. *Between Witness and Testimony: The Holocaust and the Limits of Representation.* Albany: SUNY, 2001.

Berry, William. *Collection of Maps of the World.* London: 1689.

Bhabha, Homi. "DissemiNation." *Nation and Narration.* Ed. Homi Bhabha. London: Routledge, 1990. 291–322.

———. *The Location of Culture.* London: Routledge, 1994.

Blunt, Alison, and Gillian Rose (eds.). *Writing Women and Space: Colonial and Postcolonial Geographies.* New York: Guilford, 1994.

Bowen, Emanuel. *A Complete System of Geography.* London: W. Innys et al, 1747.

Boydston, Jeanne. *Home and Work: Housework, Wages, and the Ideology of Labor in the Early Republic.* New York: Oxford UP, 1990.

Brandon, George. *Santería from Africa to the New World: The Dead Sell Memories.* Bloomington: Indiana UP, 1993.

Brathwaite, Kamau. "Interview." *Hambone* 9 (1991): 42–59.

Brown, Isabel Zakrzewski. "Historiographic Metafiction in *In the Time of the Butterflies.*" *South Atlantic Review* 64.2 (Spring 1999): 98–112.

Cambeira, Alan. *Quisqueya La Bella: The Dominican Republic in Historical and Cultural Perspective.* Armonk, NY: M. E. Sharpe, 1997.

Caminero-Santangelo, Marta. "Contesting Boundaries of Exile in Latino/a Literature." *World Literature Today* 74.3 (Summer 2000): 507–17.

Canclini, Néstor García. *Hybrid Cultures: Strategies for Entering and Leaving Modernity.* Trans. Christopher L. Chiappari and Silvia L. López. Minneapolis: U of Minnesota P, 1995.

Cardona, Nicolás de. *Spagnola*. 1632. Facsimile of the 1632 manuscript held by the Biblioteca Nacional (Madrid). Los Angeles: Dawson's Book Shop, 1974.

Carr, E. H. *The Romantic Exiles*. New York: Frederick A. Stokes, 1933.

Carter, Paul. *The Road to Botany Bay: An Essay in Spatial History*. London: Faber and Faber, 1987.

Charlevoix, P.F.X. *Histoire d'Isle Espagnole ou S Domingue*. Paris: Didot, 1731.

Ciria, Concepción Bados. "*In the Time of the Butterflies* by Julia Alvarez: History, Fiction, Testimonio and the Dominican Republic." *Monographic Review/Revista Monografica* 13 (1997): 406–16.

Cisneros, Sandra. *The House on Mango Street*. New York: Vintage, 1984.

Cofer, Judith Ortiz. *Call Me María*. New York: Orchard, 2004.

Cohen, Ralph. "History and Genre." *New Literary History* 17 (Winter 1986): 203–23.

Coronelli, Marco Vincenzo. *Archipelague du Mexique*. Venice: Dom Padovani, 1688.

Crane, Susan. "Memory, Distortion, and History in the Museum." *History and Theory* 36.4 (1997): 44–63.

———. "(Not) Writing History: Rethinking the Intersections of Personal History and Collective Memory with Hans von Aufsess." *History and Memory* 8.1 (1996): 5–29.

———. "Writing the Individual Back into Collective Memory." *American Historical Review* 102.5 (December 1997): 1372–85.

Crang, Mike. "Relics, Places and Unwritten Geographies in the Work of Michel de Certeau (1925–86)." *Thinking Space*. Ed. Mike Crang and Nigel Thrift. London: Routledge, 2000. 136–53.

Crang, Mike, and Nigel Thrift, eds. *Thinking Space*. London: Routledge, 2000.

Criado, Miryam. "Lenguaje y Otredad Sexual/Cultural en *How the García Girls Lost Their Accents* de Julia Alvarez." *The Bilingual Review/La Revista Bilingüe* 23.3 (September-December 1998): 195–205.

Danticat, Edwidge. *Behind the Mountains*. New York: Orchard, 2002.

———. *The Farming of Bones*. New York: Penguin, 1998.

Dash, J. Michael. *The Other America: Caribbean Literature in a New World Context*. Charlottesville, VA: U of Virginia P, 1998.

Davies, Carole Boyce, and Elaine Savory Fido. *Out of the KUMBLA: Caribbean Women and Literature*. Trenton, NJ: African World P, 1990.

Dayan, Joan. *Haiti, History, and the Gods*. Berkeley: U of California P, 1995.

———. "Vodoun, or the Voice of the Gods." *Raritan* 10.3 (Winter 1991): 32.

Deleuze, Gilles, and Félix Guattari. *A Thousand Plateaus: Capitalism and Schizophrenia*. Trans. Brian Massumi. Minneapolis: U of Minnesota P, 1987.

Delgadillo, Theresa. "Forms of Chicana Feminist Resistance: Hybrid Spirituality in Ana Castillo's *So Far From God*." *Modern Fiction Studies* 44.4 (1998): 888–916.

DeLoughrey, Elizabeth. "Tidalectics: Charting Caribbean 'Peoples of the Sea.'" *SPAN* 47 (October 1998): 18–38.

Desmangles, Leslie G. *The Faces of the Gods: Vodou and Roman Catholicism in Haiti.* Chapel Hill: U of North Carolina P, 1992.

Doyle, Jacqueline. "More Room of Her Own: Sandra Cisneros's *The House on Mango Street.*" *MELUS* 19.4 (Winter 1994): 5–35.

Driver, Tom F. *Liberating Rites: Understanding the Transformative Power of Ritual.* Boulder, CO: Westview, 1997.

Eichner, Bill. *The New Family Cookbook.* White River Junction, VT: Chelsea Green, 2000.

Eschevarría, Roberto González. "Sisters in Death." Rev. of *In the Time of the Butterflies,* by Julia Alvarez. *New York Times Book Review* 18 Dec. 1994: 28.

Farmer, Paul. *The Uses of Haiti.* Monroe, ME: Common Courage, 1994.

Fentress, James and Chris Wickham. *Social Memory.* Cambridge, MA: Blackwell, 1992.

Fine, Ellen S. "The Absent Memory: The Act of Writing in Post-Holocaust French Literature." *Writing and the Holocaust.* Ed. Berel Lang. New York: Holmes and Meier, 1988. 41–57.

Foucault, Michel. *Language, Counter-Memory, Practice.* Trans. Donald Bouchard and Sherry Simon. Oxford: Blackwell, 1977.

Friedman, Susan Stanford. *Mappings: Feminism and the Cultural Geographies of Encounter.* Princeton: Princeton UP, 1998.

Gaddis, John Lewes. *The Landscape of History.* Oxford: Oxford UP, 2002.

García, Cristina. *Dreaming in Cuban.* New York: Ballantine, 1993.

Garza, Melita Marie. "Sharing Secrets." *Chicago Tribune* 21 Nov. 1994: E5+.

Gilbert, Sandra M. and Susan Gubar. *The Madwoman in the Attic. The Woman Writer and the Nineteenth-Century Literary Imagination.* New Haven: Yale UP, 1979.

Gilmore, Leigh. *Autobiographics: A Feminist Theory of Women's Self-Representation.* Ithaca: Cornell UP, 1994.

Glazier, Stephen D. "Syncretism and Separation: Ritual Change in an Afro-Caribbean Faith." *Journal of American Folklore* 98.387 (1985): 49–62.

Glissant, Edouard. *Caribbean Discourse: Selected Essays.* Trans. Michael Dash. Charlottesville, VA: Caraf, 1992.

Gómez-Vega, Ibis. "Hating the Self in the 'Other' or How Yolanda Learns to See Her Own Kind in Julia Alvarez's *How the García Girls Lost Their Accents.*" *Intertexts* 3.1 (Spring 1999): 85–96.

Hall, R. A. *Haitian Creole.* Philadelphia: American Folklore Society, 1953.

Harding, Bertita. *The Land Columbus Loved Best: The Dominican Republic.* New York: Coward-McCann, 1949.

Harley, J. B., and David Woodward (eds.). *The History of Cartography.* Chicago: U of Chicago P, 1987.

Heilbrun, Carolyn. *Women's Lives: The View from the Threshold.* Toronto: U of Toronto P, 1999.

Hoffman, Joan M. "'She Wants to Be Called Yolanda Now': Identity, Language, and the Third Sister in *How the García Girls Lost Their Accents.*" *The Bilingual Review/La Revista Bilingüe* 23.1 (January–April 1998): 21–27.

Holguín, Fernando Valerio. "*En el Tiempo de las Mariposas* de Julia Alvarez: Una reinterpretación de la historia." *Chasqui* 27.1 (May 1998): 92–102.

Holloway, Julian, and James Kneale. "Mikhail Bakhtin: Dialogics of Space." *Thinking Space.* Ed. Mike Crang and Nigel Thrift. London: Routledge, 2000. 71–88.

hooks, bell. "Homeplace: A Site of Resistance." *Yearning: Race, Gender and Cultural Politics.* Boston: South End, 1990. 41–49.

Howard, David. *Coloring the Nation: Race and Ethnicity in the Dominican Republic.* Oxford: Signal, 2001.

Hunt, Lynn. *The Family Romance of the French Revolution.* Berkeley: U of California P, 1992.

Huyssen, Andreas. *Twilight Memories: Marking Time in a Culture of Amnesia.* New York: Routledge, 1995.

Jarvis, Brian. *Postmodern Cartographies: The Geographical Imagination in Contemporary American Culture.* New York: St. Martin's, 1998.

Jefferys, Thomas. *The Natural and Civil History of the French Dominion in North and South America.* London: T. Jefferys, 1760.

Johnson, Kelli Lyon. "Both Sides of the Massacre: Collective Memory and Narrative on Hispaniola." *Mosaic* 36.2 (June 2003): 75–91.

———. "Violence in the Borderlands: Crossing to the Home Space in the Novels of Ana Castillo." *Frontiers* 25:1 (Spring 2004).

Jones, Deborah. "Alvarez Brews Up Coffee with a Social Conscience." *Middlebury Campus* 10 Oct. 2001. 7 April 2004 <http://www.middleburycampus.com/main.cfm?include=detail&storyid=115346>

Kaminsky, Amy K. *After Exile: Writing the Latin American Diaspora.* Minneapolis: U of Minnesota P, 1999.

Kaplan, Caren. "Deterritorialization: The Rewriting of Home and Exile in Western Feminist Discourse." *The Nature and Context of Minority Discourse.* Ed. Abdul R. JanMohamed and David Lloyd. Oxford: Oxford UP, 1990. 357–68.

Kerber, Linda. "The Republican Mother: Women and the Enlightenment." *American Quarterly* 28.2 (1976): 187–205.

Kevane, Bridget, and Juanita Heredia. "Citizen of the World: An Interview with Julia Alvarez." *Latina Self-Portraits: Interviews with Contemporary Women Writers.* Albuquerque: U of New Mexico P, 2000. 19–32. Kirby, Kathleen. *Indifferent Boundaries: Spatial Concepts of Human Subjectivity.* New York: Guilford, 1996.

Klein, Kerwin Lee. "Grounds for Remembering: On the Emergence of Memory in Historical Discourse." *Representations* 69 (2000): 127–50.

Knight, Franklin. "The Historical Unity of the Caribbean." *The Process of Unity in Caribbean Society: Ideologies and Literature.* Ed. Ileana Rodriguez and Marc

Zimmerman. Minneapolis: Institute for the Study of Ideologies and Literature, 1983. 58–64.

Labat, Jean Baptiste. *Nouvelle voyages aux isles de l'Amerique.* Paris: CavalierG, 1722.

Laet, Joannes de. *Histoire du Nouveau Monde.* Leyden: Elsevier, 1640.

Lanza, Carmela Delia. "Hearing Voices: Women and Home and Ana Castillo's *So Far From God.*" *MELUS* 23.1 (Spring 1998): 65–79.

Larsen, Neil. "¿Como narrar el trujillato?" *Revista Iberoamericana* 54.1–2 (Jan–March 1988): 89–98.

Lashgari, Deidre (ed.). *Violence, Silence, and Anger: Women's Writing as Transgression.* Charlottesville: UP of Virginia, 1995.

Lefebvre, Henri. *The Production of Space.* Trans. Donald Nicholson-Smith. Oxford: Blackwell, 1991.

Loriggio, Francesco. "Regionalism and Theory." *Regionalism Reconsidered: New Approaches to the Field.* Ed. David Jordan. New York: Garland, 1994. 3–27.

Luis, William. *Dance between Two Cultures: Latino Caribbean Literature Written in the United States.* Nashville: Vanderbilt UP, 1997.

Lyons, Bonnie, and Bill Oliver. "A Clean Windshield: Julia Alvarez." *Passion and Craft: Conversations with Notable Writers.* Urbana: U of Illinois P, 1998. 128–44.

Maher, Susan Nanamore. "Deep Mapping the Great Plains: Surveying the Literary Cartography of Place." *Western American Literature* 36.1 (2001): 4–25.

Marcus, Jane. "Alibis and Legends: The Ethics of Elsewhereness, Gender and Estrangement." *Women's Writing in Exile.* Ed. Mary Lynn Broe and Angela Ingram. Chapel Hill: U of North Carolina P, 1989. 269–94.

Martínez, Elizabeth Coonrod. "Recovering Space for History between Imperialism and Patriarchy: Julia Alvarez's *In the Time of the Butterflies.*" *Thamyris* 5.2 (Autumn 1998): 263–79.

Massey, Doreen. *Space, Place, and Gender.* Minneapolis: U of Minnesota P, 1994.

Mayock, Ellen C. "The Bicultural Construction of Self in Cisneros, Alvarez, and Santiago." *The Bilingual Review/La Revista Bilingüe* 23.3 (September–December 1998): 223–29.

McCracken, Ellen. *New Latina Narrative: The Feminine Space of Postmodern Ethnicity.* Tucson: U of Arizona P, 1999.

Milosz, Czeslaw. "Notes on Exile." *Altogether Elsewhere: Writers on Exile.* Ed. Marc Robinson. New York: Harcourt Brace, 1994. 36–40.

Mir, Pedro. *Amén de Mariposas.* Santo Domingo: Nuevo Mundo, 1969.

Moraga, Cherríe. *Loving in the War Years.* Boston: South End, 1983.

Murdoch, H. Adlai. *Creole Identity in the French Caribbean Novel.* Gainesville: UP of Florida, 2001.

Nanita, Abelardo R. *Trujillo: The Biography of a Great Leader.* New York: Vantage, 1957.

Nodelman, Perry. "Pleasure and Genre: Speculations on the Characteristics of Children's Fiction." *Children's Literature 28*. New Haven: Yale UP, 2000.1–14.

Nora, Pierre. "Between Memory and History: *Les Lieux de Mémoire*." *Representations* 26 (Spring 1989): 7–24.

Olivares, Julian. "Sandra Cisneros's *The House on Mango Street* and the Poetics of Space." *Chicana Creativity and Criticism: New Frontiers in American Literature*. Ed. María Herrera-Sobek and Helena María Viramontes. Albuquerque: U of New Mexico P, 1996. 233–44.

Ostriker, Alicia. "The Thieves of Language: Women Poets and Revisionist Mythmaking." *Signs* 8.1 (Autumn 1982): 68–90.

Paravisini-Gebert, Lizabeth. "Women against the Grain: The Pitfalls of Theorizing Caribbean Women's Writing." *Winds of Change: The Transforming Voices of Caribbean Women Writers and Scholars*. Ed. Adele S. Newson and Linda Strong-Leek. New York: Peter Lang, 1998. 161–68.

Paravisini, Lizabeth, and Barbara Webb. "On the Threshold of Becoming Caribbean Women Writers." *Cimarron* 1.3 (1988): 106–31.

Perkins, Thelma. "Children Should Be Seen and Spoken To: Or . . . Writing for and about Children." *Framing the Word: Gender and Genre in Caribbean Women's Writing*. Ed. Joan Anim-Addo. London: Whiting and Birch, 1996. 103–7.

Phillips, Judith Wingerd. *A Partial Grammar of the Haitian Creole Verb System: Form, Function, and Syntax*. Dissertation at SUNY Buffalo, 1982. Reprinted by University Microfilms International.

Piper, Karen. "Post-Colonialism in the United States: Diversity or Hybridity?" *Postcolonial Literatures: Expanding the Canon*. Ed. Deborah L. Madsen. London: Pluto, 1999. 14–28.

Ponce, Nicolas. *Recueil de vues de Saint-Domingue*. Paris: Moreau, 1791.

Puleo, Gus. "Remembering and Reconstructing the Mirabal Sisters in Julia Alvarez's *In the Time of the Butterflies*." *The Bilingual Review/La Revista Bilingüe* 23.1 (January–April 1998): 11–20.

Pulley, Raymond H. "The United States and the Trujillo Dictatorship, 1933–1940: The High Price of Caribbean Stability." *Caribbean Studies* 5.1 (1965): 22–31.

Rabe, Stephen G. "The Caribbean Triangle: Betancourt, Castro, and Trujillo and U.S. Foreign Policy, 1958–1963." *Diplomatic History* 20.1 (1996): 55–78.

Rich, Adrienne. "Notes toward a Politics of Location." *Blood, Bread and Poetry: Selected Prose, 1979–1985*. New York: Norton, 1986. 210–32.

Rogoff, Irit. "From Ruins to Debris: The Feminization of Fascism in German History Museums." *Museum Culture: Histories, Discourses, Spectacles*. Ed. Daniel J. Sherman and Irit Rogoff. Minneapolis: U of Minnesota P, 1994.

Roorda, Eric. *The Dictator Next Door: The Good Neighbor Policy and the Trujillo Regime in the Dominican Republic, 1930–1945*. Durham: Duke UP, 1998.

Rosario-Sievert, Heather. "Conversation with Julia Alvarez." *Review: Latin American Literature and Arts* (Spring 1997): 31–37.

Rose, Gillian. *Feminism and Geography*. Minneapolis: U of Minnesota P, 1993.

Said, Edward. "Reflections on Exile." *Out There: Marginalization and Contemporary Cultures*. Ed. Russell Ferguson. New York: The New Museum of Contemporary Art and Massachusetts Institute of Technology, 1990. 357–66.

———. *The World, the Text, and the Critic*. Cambridge, MA: Harvard UP, 1983.

Saldívar-Hull, Sonia. *Feminism on the Border: Chicana Gender Politics and Literature*. Berkeley: U of California P, 2000.

Santiago, Esmeralda. *When I Was Puerto Rican*. New York: Vintage, 1994.

Savory, Elaine. "En/Gendering Spaces: The Poetry of Marlene Nourbese Philip and Pamela Mordecai." *Framing the Word: Gender and Genre in Caribbean Women's Writing*. Ed. Joan Anim-Addo. London: Whiting and Birch, 1996. 12–27.

———. "Ex/Isle: Separation, Memory, and Desire in Caribbean Women's Writing." *Winds of Change: The Transforming Voices of Caribbean Women Writers and Scholars*. Ed. Adele S. Newson and Linda Strong-Leek. New York: Peter Lang, 1998. 169–77.

Sawyer, R. Keith. "The Semiotics of Improvisation: The Pragmatics of Musical and Verbal Performance." *Semiotica* 108.3–4 (1996): 269–306.

Shihab Nye, Naomi. "My Grandmother in the Stars." *Red Suitcase*. Brockport, NY: BOA Editions, 1994. 41.

Shudson, Michael. "Dynamics of Distortion in Collective Memory." *Memory Distortion: How Minds, Brains, and Societies Reconstruct the Past*. Ed. Daniel L. Schachter. Cambridge, MA: Harvard UP, 1995. 346–64.

Smith-Rosenberg, Carroll. "The Female World of Love and Ritual: Relations between Women in Nineteenth-Century America." *Signs* 1975 1(1): 1–30.

Stefanko, Jacqueline. "New Ways of Telling: Latinas' Narratives of Exile and Return." *Frontiers* 17.2 (1996): 50–69.

Suárez, Isabel Carrera. "Hyphens, Hybridities, and Mixed-Race Identities: Gendered Readings in Contemporary Canadian Women's Texts." *Caught Between Cultures: Women, Writing and Subjectivities*. Ed. Elizabeth Russell. Amsterdam: Rodopi, 2002. 15–33.

Taylor, Patrick. "Dancing the Nation." *Nation Dance: Religion, Identity, and Difference in the Caribbean*. Ed. Patrick Taylor. Bloomington: Indiana UP, 2001. 1–13.

Todorov, Tzvetan. *Genres in Discourse*. Trans. Catherine Porter. Cambridge: Cambridge UP, 1990.

Torres-Saillant, Silvio. "On Conceptualizing Caribbean Literature." *Annals of Scholarship: an International Quarterly in the Humanities & Social Sciences* 10.2 (1993): 219–27.

Tuan, Yi-Fu. *Space and Place: The Perspective of Experience*. Minneapolis: U of Minnesota P, 1977.

Ureña, Salomé. *Poesías Completas*. Santo Domingo: ONAP, 1985.

Veciano-Suárez, Ana. *Flight to Freedom*. New York: Orchard, 2002.

"Warning Beneath the Cliff." *Time* 12 Dec. 1960: 32.

Welter, Barbara. "The Cult of True Womanhood: 1820–1860." *American Quarterly* 18 (1966): 151–74.

Wiley, Catherine. "Interview." *The Bloomsbury Review* 12.2 (March 1992): 9–10.

"Wives of 3 Foes of Trujillo Dead." *New York Times* 30 Nov. 1960: 5.

Wucker, Michele. *Why the Cocks Fight: Dominicans, Haitians, and the Struggle for Hispaniola*. New York: Hill and Wang, 2000.

Young, Robert J. C. *Colonial Desire: Hybridity in Theory, Culture, and Race*. London: Routledge, 1995.

Index

COMPLETE COPYRIGHT CREDITS